The Life

and Death of a

Minke Whale in

the Amazon:

Dispatches

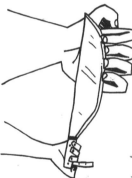

from the

Brazilian

Rainforest

The Life

and Death of a

Minke Whale in

the Amazon:

Dispatches

from the

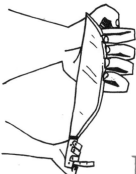

Brazilian

Rainforest

Fábio Zuker

translated from the Portuguese by **Ezra E. Fitz**

MILKWEED EDITIONS

Published 2022 by Milkweed Editions
Printed in the United States of America
Cover design by Mary Austin Speaker
Cover art and interior art by Gustavo Caboco
Map by Katie Lukes
Author photo by Fábio Zuker
22 23 24 25 26   5 4 3 2 1
First Edition

Library of Congress Cataloging-in-Publication Data

Names: Zuker, Fábio, author. | Fitz, Ezra E., translator.
Title: The life and death of a minke whale in the Amazon : and other stories of the Brazilian rainforest / Fábio Zuker ; translated from the Portuguese by Ezra E. Fitz.
Other titles: Vida e morte de uma baleia-minke no interior do Pará e outras histórias da Amazônia. English
Description: Minneapolis, Minnesota : Milkweed Editions, 2021. | Summary: "A collection of essays on life and Indigenous resistance in the Amazon rainforest during an age of raging wildfires, mass migration, populist politics, and increasing deforestation"-- Provided by publisher.
Identifiers: LCCN 2021011585 (print) | LCCN 2021011586 (ebook) | ISBN 9781571311818 (paperback) | ISBN 9781571317537 (ebook)
Subjects: LCSH: Rain forest conservation--Amazon River Region. | Rain forests--Brazil. | LCGFT: Essays.
Classification: LCC PQ9698.436.U54 V5313 2021 (print) | LCC PQ9698.436.U54 (ebook) | DDC 869.4/5--dc23
LC record available at https://lccn.loc.gov/2021011585
LC ebook record available at https://lccn.loc.gov/2021011586

Milkweed Editions is committed to ecological stewardship. We strive to align our book production practices with this principle, and to reduce the impact of our operations in the environment. We are a member of the Green Press Initiative, a nonprofit coalition of publishers, manufacturers, and authors working to protect the world's endangered forests and conserve natural resources. *The Life and Death of a Minke Whale in the Amazon* was printed by McNaughton & Gunn.

CONTENTS

The Life

and Death of a

Minke Whale in

the Amazon:

Dispatches

from the

Brazilian

Rainforest

THE BRAZILIAN AMAZON

1. Marajó
2. Altamira
3. Santarém
4. Manaus
5. Anamã
6. Boa Vista
7. São Gabriel
   da Cachoeira

Introduction:
Writing as the Projection of Worlds

During one of her recent stays with the Indigenous Wari' people, in 2014, Aparecida Vilaça was impressed by something of a novelty: several photographs of her Wari' friends and relatives covered one of the bedroom walls. It was in the home of Paletó, her Indigenous father, with whom Aparecida had been developing a relationship since 1986, when she began anthropological fieldwork with the Wari' in the northern state of Rondônia. The pictures showed several Indigenous people in Western garb, including Davi, who suffered from atrophy of the legs, and who was photographed standing next to his sister Ja. Intrigued, Aparecida asked Ja if they had bought those clothes. No, Ja replied. They'd been photoshopped by a specialist from Guajará-Mirim, a town not far from the Wari' villages.

Reflecting on this, Aparecida analyzes the way photography was appropriated by the Wari', "not in terms of permanence or stability, of mirroring the world, but in terms of transformation, of projecting bodies into another world." Her book, *Paletó and Me: Memories of My Indigenous Father*, can be read through the lens of this Wari' principle of projecting bodies into other worlds. It's an attempt to recreate the Indigenous Paletó somewhere else: the world of the living, the world of white people, the world of books, while exploring a relationship of caring and affection. In the book, Paletó appears as a collage of excerpts from the author's field notebooks, dreams, and personal memories, as well as from transcripts of cassette tapes, conversations, and others' memories of him.

Produced over thirty years, this multifaceted material is the basis for a kind of farewell to Paletó. The book opens the day after his death, emotionally narrated by the author as she shares her anguish at being separated from her Indigenous father and unable to follow his funeral despite many attempts to establish virtual or phone contact with her Wari' brothers and sisters.

The projection of bodies into another world is a feature of Wari' thought especially with regard to their concept of what photography can do. It's a reflection that takes us beyond a specific context. Sending images of bodies and people into another world, projecting worlds over other worlds, and bringing different realities into friction is what I hope to do with the reports and stories in this book.

More than simply transposing texts for people, recreating them in a different world, it is more interesting to think about how their ways of life test the limits of a record intended to account for the world into which these people are inviting us. What strikes me is the way a text always seems insufficient when faced with a reality that stretches our narrative capacity to grasp it.

A figure comes to mind: something that cannot be embraced. Something with a certain dynamic, a flow that corrodes from within every form or structure designed to contain it. A dynamic, somewhere between fluidity and containment, from which the following stories certainly will not escape. Or, more accurately, it is precisely through this friction that they may emerge.

A Forest in Flames

As I'm writing this, it's still 2019. The year is not over, but it can already be considered a catastrophic one for the Brazilian Amazon. I spent much of it in the Tupinambá village of Cabeceira do Amorim, inside the Tapajós-Arapiuns Extractive Reserve in western Pará. Nearly every night, Ezeriel and I would watch *Jornal Nacional* in the living room of his home, a place of unplastered walls and usually crisscrossed with hammocks of the most diverse colors, sizes, and shapes. There isn't even a bed in the room Ezeriel shares with his wife, the *cacica* Estevina, an important Indigenous leader. His sons and daughters have already left the nest and started families of their own. Some live in the city of Santarém while others moved to Manaus or Macapá. Many still live in the village and have become excellent hunters. Every night they return to their childhood home with their spouses and children, bringing fish and game to share for dinner.

A few of them join Ezeriel and me as we watch the news of the surge in deforestation currently taking place in the Amazon, our mouths agape. Ezeriel raises an eyebrow. The director of Brazil's National Institute for Space Research (INPE), which is also responsible for monitoring forest fires and other destructions of rainforest habitat, was on a national network calling President Jair Bolsonaro "pusillanimous and cowardly" after the president questioned the institute data. Since the beginning, his administration has been dismantling Brazil's environmental protection agencies. Quietly, as if holding something back, Ezeriel mentioned that loggers were looking to resume their activities inside the reserve, which he and many other Indigenous Tupinambá and Kumaruara people claim as ancestral territory.

These are the same logging companies that have been devastating the Tupinambá territory, as well as that of other Indigenous and riverside peoples in the region, for decades. Now they even have the support of some local residents, and logging has resumed to the east, in Nova Canãa. The Tupinambá, with their twenty villages, are concerned, which is why they want to mark the boundaries of their territory clearly, to manage it autonomously and expel the loggers. But the wind is not at the backs of those striving to defend the rivers and rainforests.

There's the data collected by satellites and there are the daily personal experiences of destruction. It is precisely in the tension between these two scales that I'm trying to write about the ongoing disaster, about the fate of the rainforest and its ways of life. Sheer numbers can't do it. They don't communicate enough to fully account for what's going on in the Amazon today.

Transforming the Rainforest into Fields of Soy

A few days after watching Bolsonaro's crusade to deregulate the lumber industry, I headed back up the river to Santarém. Roughly ten hours by boat. The Tapajós is a wide river, and the confluence where it joins with the Amazon and Arapiuns, in the so-called Lago Grande, has an oceanic feel. You are a speck in the middle of the sea, even while you're in the heart of the largest rainforest on the planet.

Here, hammocks tend to get tangled on deck. Whenever there's a storm, or when the wind picks up a bit, which isn't uncommon, it's important to hold fast to the gunwales or some other sturdy piece of wood. Otherwise, the to-and-fro of the waves makes it all but impossible not to get tossed out. I usually take advantage of times like this where I'm more or less unplugged to chat with people, to sleep, or to read. This time, however, a strange burning smell had me on alert. I also thought I saw a bit of smoke coming from the other bank, beyond the Tapajós National Forest. At the time I had no idea of just how massive the fire actually was, spreading along the BR-163 highway, which connects Cuiabá, the state capital of Mato Grosso, with Santarém.

On board our boat, the smell of burning brush sparked a conversation, but from our point of view, traveling along a vast river from distant Indigenous villages towards the city, the smokiness in the air seemed like small-scale, controlled fires. A few days later, news of the increasing number of fires in the Amazon spread across the globe: a direct consequence of the incentives created by Bolsonaro's criminal actions. Like smoldering embers left after a blaze, the hot spots on the radar were concentrated in an "arc of deforestation," which stretched from the state of Rondônia to Santarém, passing through southern Amazonas.

The expansion of soy production in the Amazon can be seen as a transformational process for the relationship between people and plants. It's about transforming the multiplicity of species in a rainforest environment into monochrome, single-crop fields. It's not a natural change, it's a sociopolitical one. A long process that involves economic agents (such as large farmers), local politicians, illegal actions (like buying land from traditional communities and protected areas), and, of course, fire. With the onset of the dry season, and the resulting drop in rainfall, the use of fire becomes the most basic means of destroying the forest.

Unlike other biomes such as the savanna, which regularly burns during the dry season as part of a recovery process, there are no natural fires in the Amazon. Once lit, they risk spreading well beyond the intended area. But every fire always follows the same life cycle: grow, spread, and convert the multiplicity of species into a single uniform substance—ash. Rich in nutrients, the ash now fertilizes the soil. The remains of the forest have become the perfect environment for the development of single-crop soy farming.

It isn't only the Amazon that's burning. In 2019, we witnessed astonishing destruction from wildfires in California, in Australia, and even in the unlikeliest of places, such as the East Siberian taiga. The idea, proposed by a number of scientists, of a new geological era known as the Pyrocene—when everything burns, from oil fields generating energy to tropical rainforests—no longer seems inappropriate.

In Tupinambá villages along the west bank of the Tapajós River, soy is considered "just" a threat. In Munduruku communities on the opposite side of the river, soy is a reality: what's left of the forest is being smothered by fields of soy. There is a bleak game of mirrors going on between the Tapajós's two banks, which are locked in step, so that what happens on the river's east bank, which is easier to access by road, is likely very soon to happen on the western side as well.

Ezeriel, Pedrinho, and João, all of them Indigenous Tupinambá, are now engaged in marking the boundaries of their territory. As the government is generally unreceptive to their petitions, they have decided to take matters into their own hands. In 2017, we set out into the jungle together. Self-demarcation consists of opening up the undergrowth with machetes and creating trails to facilitate inspections. As part of the team, my job was to operate the GPS device and to write about the undertaking in hopes of drawing some attention to it. I'd had some experience as a reporter, but was of little use with the GPS. The Tupinambá were guided by the movement of the clouds. Despite often asking them to explain how they did this, I never fully understood. All I can say is that the clouds have regular patterns of movement depending on the size of the river. This fluctuation was enough for the Indigenous people to establish their route, bypassing neighboring villages. "That way!" they would point. And I would be staring into a dense thicket, unable to imagine how we would penetrate that profusion of razor grass, weeds, and other "pernicious herbage" that, wrapped as it was around the trunks of larger trees, seemed to constitute an impenetrable barrier.

But that wasn't always the case. "If you think about it, I was a deforester myself," Pedrinho said to me. João, for his part, retains a certain pride in having hunted a lot in this jungle to feed workers at the Santa Izabel lumber company. He looks back on those days as the golden age of his youth, when he earned one salary cutting down wood and another as a huntsman. "I was the one supporting those workers," he remarks while prepping manioc flour for sale in the city.

In fact, the entire Tupinambá village of Cabeceira do Amorim, and many of the surrounding communities, seems to have worked for Santa Izabel at some point. The Indigenous people have a distinct memory of how the company operated before it retreated from the region when the extractive reserve was created in 1998. They used to cut down large trees, including *ipês*, *mandioqueiras*, angelins, and *melancieiras*. But according to João, despite the logging company's extracting trees for years, over two-thirds of that forest is still standing to this day.

It's hard to picture anything more perverse than a private economic agent using a scheme of seduction to transform people who depend on a certain territory into their own predators.

Little by little, the Tupinambá began to realize that the forest was disappearing, and with it, the game. Despite the bit of money they earned working for the company, the devastation it was creating would soon make life in the region impossible for Indigenous people. They would depend more and more on the city for everything from food to medicine. And the disappearing jungle presented another problem: life in the city is expensive. The contrast between life in the villages and life in the urban areas was put in stark relief by *cacica* Estevina: "Here, the rainforest gives us everything: our food, our game, our garden. In the city, everything comes with a price. If you're twenty cents short for a medicine, nobody will sell it to you."

Along the meandering course of the Tapajós, the peoples, the rivers, and the rainforest have established a codependency, a relationship of mutual formation. These are not Indigenous people who happen to live in a particular territory, but people whose bodies are formed (to the extent that their bodies, too, constitute territories) by hunting, visiting relatives, planting, and healing through their herbalist. This process is evident in both the ancestral knowledge and the geological formations themselves, such as the ancient anthropogenic land known as the *terra preta* or "Indian black earth."

Lacking income, and with the depredation of their forests, the Tupinambá were surely going to be integrated into modern Brazilian society. But this integration would take place at the lowest level possible. Megaron Txucarramãe is one of the most eminent Indigenous leaders in the country. A member of the Kayapó people inhabiting the Xingu basin, he rose to prominence as a staunch opponent of the Belo Monte Hydroelectric Dam constructed in the northern part of the Xingu River. I interviewed him in 2018 during the Acampamento Terra Livre ("Free Land Camp"), which took place around the same time that Bolsonaro was gaining traction in Brazil's presidential race. "If he integrates the Indian into white society, the Indian will be worse off than the people who live in the favelas, the people who have no land, no roof over their heads," he said. "Many Indians have no training or education with which to support their family (in the cities). In the villages, on his own land, the Indian knows how to do the things he has traditionally learned and has continued doing to this very day. On his land, in his place." The Kayapó *cacique* then offers a warning: "Integrate the Indian into society? The Indian will die, the Indian will cease to exist!"

In communities like Piquiatuba, which is on the east bank of the Tapajós River and within the Tapajós National Forest, reality is very different from what the Tupinambá are experiencing. Fields of soy surround the rainforest. Remerson Castro Almeida, a community leader responsible for running the local inn and cleaning the school, rightly fears that what's left of the forest will eventually be replaced by soy. "It's much hotter here than it used to be, and we're starting to see insects in the community that we've never seen before," he says, suspecting that the use of pesticides is driving wildlife out of the jungle and into the villages along the river. In an ever hotter world, soybean fields are true heat-producing machines. Increasing temperatures sweep across the roughly fifty kilometers of forest that separates Remerson from the fields, making routine outdoor work more difficult, which in turn reduces production. Before, they could work the land until noon; today, by ten thirty, nobody can stand the heat.

The Tapajós National Forest was created by Decree No. 73,684, on February 19, 1974, during Brazil's military dictatorship (1964–1985). Spanning 527,319 hectares, it encompasses the municipalities of Belterra, Aveiro, Placas, and Rurópolis, all in the state of Pará. It therefore harbors roughly 5,000 residents, of which about 500 are Indigenous. The government had a single goal: to clear the forest of people; to make the sexist western image of a "virgin forest" into a reality. The military wanted to ship all the Indigenous people living there off to the Cachimbo Mountains like cargo—and did exactly that with several Indigenous populations elsewhere in the Amazon.

Seu Milton remembers in great detail the struggle to remain there, although he does regret that, with the creation of the Conservation Unit, he can't sell his land to large corporate farms. On the other hand, he calls attention to the abundance of fauna that once lived in the forest: "There was a lot of hunting back then, mostly deer and small game. There was a lot of fishing, too, both with rods and by bow-and-arrow. Now, I don't think there's a single peccary left. They all ran away from the falling trees." Seu Tarcilo, who was also active in the movement to keep residents in the jungle, today finds himself more aligned with the Bolsonaro administration. To him, Brazil's Institute of the Environment and Renewable Natural Resources (IBAMA) and the Chico Mendes Institute for Biodiversity Conservation (ICMBio) "did a lot of harm—a whole lot of harm—to the development of the people living along the Tapajós. Everything came grinding to a halt!" He goes on to talk about the fines for environmental crimes, which Bolsonaro denounced as an "industry" that needs to be shut down, and he believes that, without the National Forest, people would be much better off with open fields dedicated to agriculture. I was especially struck by one thing he said: "When the light comes in, you stop having those old visions." The ghosts have gone.

I am determined to reflect on the destruction of myriad forms of life in the Lower Tapajós River Basin, starting with the relationship between people and plants. Plants aren't just there to be used according to human interest. Plants make worlds. They are creators of realities. The Indigenous people in this region have established a tightly-woven relationship, a true sphere of kinship, with the vegetation around them—not merely a utilitarian one. Their practices, the mutually reliant arrangement they have with the land, call into question the concept of human exceptionalism, of people as separate from the world around them, which is theirs to dominate. In fact, the plants themselves offer a mediation between the land and the people; the plants alone make it possible for the two old opponents to coexist, imposing on our language the challenge of describing their relationship as between nonopposing parts.

There is a geopolitical aspect to soy, distinguished by its colonizing momentum. But there is also a cosmopolitical war over soy, one capable of creating and destroying people, and even worlds. Pure fields of grain don't exist in nature. Whether accidental or planned, the ancient tradition of farming and harvesting grain is now part of a political strategy that exacerbates the concentration of power. It benefits both parties: the farmers' wealth increases, and the reproduction of the selected crop is guaranteed to a dizzying degree. Along the Tapajós, this desire for multiplication is transforming the landscape. A shipping port and related infrastructure is required, including the dredging of river bottoms to make shipping the harvested soybeans possible. This destroys breeding grounds for fish. Soy craves land and requires the destruction of other species. Once tamed, it will tame others. Without places for fish to spawn naturally, commercial fish farms flourish. Soy is in constant conflict with humans. Large-scale farmers will, at any cost—and the costs are very high indeed—try to bend and conform it to their commercial objectives, managing it with toxic chemicals in order to defend it from all that may stand in their way. From a pesticidal point of view, insects, Indigenous people, and traditional ways of life are equal: they are no more than obstacles to be surmounted.

The Indigenous struggle is not merely for existence but for a different existence: not to let themselves be absorbed into an all-encompassing white culture. The "mono" of soybean monoculture must be taken seriously as a political bid to eradicate all difference. In this sense, the rainforest emerges as the Indigenous peoples' greatest ally.

Elegy to an Amazonian River

Sometimes I find myself thinking of this text as an elegy. But not for long. An elegy is a farewell, an expression of regret in the name of someone who has gone—whether dead or distant—leaving behind the person who is writing. To call this text an elegy to the Tapajós River would be like signing its death certificate . . . which is not within my power.

But there is no shortage of reasons to suspect that the river is dying. Or, rather, that it's being murdered. Hydroelectric plants, gold mining, deforestation, and dredging, to name just a few. As a landscape, the Lower Tapajós River Basin is as natural as any human construct.

Dona Teca, one of the oldest residents of Piquiatuba, can see the river from her home. We enjoy the sunset together from her wide-open kitchen overlooking the waters. At night, we sleep, rocking to the rhythm of the waves. In contrast with the serenity of the moment, she laments the effects hydroelectric dams have had on the river and on her life. She fears an increase in diseases and the departure of local fish populations. "The river has changed color," she remarks. "It's darker." No response comes to mind. I remain silent.

Brazilians and Venezuelans:
A Chronicle of Hatred
and Compassion

"Of course I always thought about visiting Brazil, going to Carnival, the beaches, catching a soccer game . . . but as a tourist. Not like this, not destitute." "You can't treat someone like this, no matter who they are!" "We're human beings. We're Venezuelans. We're coming here and people have to understand the situation back home is unbearable." "Did you know there's a blockade on Venezuela? Of course things are bad, the government is inept and corrupt, but it only got to this point with the economic blockade." "The point of all this is to sow fear in the country, to humiliate people, to make the world see the extent of the problems in Venezuela." "I just want to thank you. I've never been short of food here." "I've been treated so well; someone even gave me a pair of boots they were wearing." "They didn't manage to kill me with sticks and stones because I kept running."

It was after ten o'clock at night when I approached a group of Venezuelans living behind the Manaus Bus Terminal. I asked if they might be willing to talk with me about their situation as migrants sleeping on the street when the temperature, even at night, was in the high eighties. After deliberating for a moment, they agreed to speak, as long as I didn't take any pictures—a request to be repeated at every interview. Of the roughly thirty people there, about half of them engaged vociferously in the conversation which, little by little, grew into a larger debate with the tone of a rally. One, Senhor Reynaldo Pérez, took the role of moderator, while the remaining half of the group continued to rest on sheets of cardboard on the ground or in hammocks. Some would approach as if about to join the conversation, before backing away again, while others contented themselves with sweeping the floor or folding the few clothes that they had. I sat on the ground in order to better participate in the discussion. It was clear that this was also a moment of collective venting, as well as of reflection on the sudden change in their lives. None of them were sure how it had happened.

A security guard and a candy and snack vendor first alerted me to the existence of a group of Venezuelans camping behind the bus station. As I was buying a bottle of water and preparing for the eleven-hour journey between Manaus and Boa Vista, my ear caught a few unflattering comments about the newly arrived immigrants. The security guard and the vendor were complaining that the Venezuelans had brought diseases such as measles and meningitis to Brazil, while the Indigenous people arriving with them, especially the Warao, were "a bunch of drifters who do nothing but ask for things."

"They're not even Indians," the vendor replied. "If they were, they'd be selling their crafts." The guard, in his beret and military-style jacket, declared, "There's only passengers here. If a vagrant shows up, I'll throw him out!"

Far from being the unique, this kind of hateful, racist speech and attitude proved less common than the global media coverage of Brazilians expelling Venezuelans in Pacaraima, a city in the northern state of Roraima that shares a border with Venezuela, would have you believe. The public discussion centers on compassion, sadness, and frustration at the inability to help more people in such a delicate situation, which coexists with racists feelings of "disgust," "dirtiness," and "danger" around the newcomers.

I met one Brazilian family with limited resources who welcomed an entire family of Venezuelans into their home, and heard of many similar stories. If the talk of hatred and violence garners more attention, it's the sense of isolation and abandonment among the citizens of Roraima that may be the key to understanding this conflict: Brazil's least populated state was bearing the brunt of a previously unimaginable flow of immigrants.

Reynaldo, the leader of our discussion behind the Manaus bus station, is also the most thoughtful member of the group. He criticizes Venezuela's president, Nicolás Maduro, as well as the opposition and the embargo on Venezuela, and also deplores the xenophobic attacks, and appreciates the reception the Venezuelans have found in Brazil. "In Brazil, you don't discuss politics like we do in Venezuela," he says, his tone at once playful and sad. "That was our downfall. . ."

With around 576,000 inhabitants (according to the 2010 census), Roraima is Brazil's least populated state. It is also the only state not connected to the national electrical grid, depending on neighboring Venezuela for its energy supply. Blackouts are frequent in the capital, Boa Vista, home to roughly 375,000 residents, due to the interruptions resulting from Venezuela's transmission failures. When these blackouts happen—I've witnessed two myself—the state's thermoelectric plants, which are much more expensive to run, kick in to compensate.

In preparation for connecting Roraima to the national grid, federal government projects include a junction to connect the state with its neighbor, Amazonas: high-tension power lines would have to cross territory belonging to the Indigenous Waimiri-Atroari people, who live on the border between the two states. The Indigenous community is vehemently opposed to this proposal. It brings back memories of the developmentalism imposed by the Brazilian dictatorship which nearly led to their extermination. Discussions are at such an impasse that the president of Brazil's National Indian Foundation (FUNAI), General Franklimberg Ribeiro Freitas, was forced out due to the difficulties of negotiating with the Indigenous people.

Electrical isolation is a perfect image for portraying Roraima's sense of separation from the rest of Brazil. Indigenous people have often been considered responsible, by local politicians and popular opinion alike, for the state's lack of development and energy, for other land rights issues. Nearly half of Roraima—46 percent—is Indigenous land.

According to Marcos Braga, professor of Indigenous and intercultural studies at the Federal University of Roraima, "this is an anti-Indigenous state, and it's become an anti-Worker's Party state due to Raposa Serra do Sol"—which is an Indigenous territory established in 2005 despite strong opposition from the non-Indigenous population. For Braga, the conflict is largely led by rice farmers forced out of the Indigenous territory and headed by Paulo César Quartiero, who was elected as a federal representative in 2010 and whose résumé includes accusations of orchestrating armed attacks on Indigenous Makuxi people. Denise Wapishana, an Indigenous leader and literature scholar, laments: "There's such great hatred towards Indigenous peoples. They're asking why the Indian wants so much land. It's just so sad to hear things like that."

As for the Venezuelan immigrants, the same scapegoat logic used against Indigenous people is now being reiterated and exploited by politicians running for reelection as well as by the local media, which is basically dominated by these same politicians. Former senator Romero Jucá of the Brazilian Democratic Movement party (MDB) is one of these. He unsuccessfully sought reelection in 2018, and his family owns the state's largest communications group, along with television affiliates Rede Bandeirantes, Rede Record, TV Imperial, as well as a print newspaper and two radio stations.

According to Professor Elói Senhoras, of the Amazonian Center for Research in International Relations, "There was already a serious problem with violence in Roraima. Considering both the influx of immigrants and the preexisting crime rate, there has been a marginal increase in violence," he added, pointing out that Roraima has the highest per capita murder rate of women and the LGBTQ+ population. Professor Senhoras further comments that, "The political discourse has resorted to painting Venezuelans as scapegoats, and the massive influx of Venezuelans is taking over the space that had been dedicated to Indigenous issues during previous campaigns."

The coexistence between the Brazilian and Venezuelan populations is not, however, defined only by conflict. Boa Vista and Pacaraima have become bilingual cities, and it's not uncommon to find Venezuelans working in virtually every aspect of the service industry alongside native Brazilians, communicating in "Portunhol." Further, many Brazilians take pride in helping the immigrants. However, if the citizens of Roraima feel that they've gone above and beyond in welcoming the Venezuelan population, the same cannot be said of Brazil's federal government, whose measures appear purely cosmetic.

In Marcos Braga's opinion, "The Brazilian government has been rather coy": while an estimated one hundred thousand Venezuelans have already crossed the border into Pacaraima since 2016, the government has only redistributed a few hundred elsewhere in Brazil and built a dozen shelters (ten in the capital, two in Pacaraima) which accommodate just over five thousand people.

"They're trying to fit an entire country into a single state" is an expression commonly heard in Roraima, and it's not an exaggeration. The arrival of one hundred thousand people represents 20 percent of the state's entire population, which is generally poor and has little capacity to create jobs. The state budget is almost entirely dependent on paychecks from the department of public services and from small businesses. Lastly, an uncomfortable relationship with the national media, which quickly labeled the people of Roraima as xenophobic, only exacerbates their sense of isolation from the rest of the country.

It's hard to come up with a specific profile of the Venezuelan immigrant who travels the roughly thirteen kilometers that separates Santa Elena de Uairén in Venezuela from Pacaraima in Brazil. What they share may simply be their escape from the misery and hunger that plagues their native land and their hope of a better life abroad, a temporary one, preferably, and the expectation of a swift return to their country of origin "when things get better" or "when they get rid of Maduro," which, for many, are one and the same.

Most of the immigrants I interviewed aren't even considering staying in Brazil permanently. They crossed the border by land, which is relatively easily done and inexpensive, with the plan of working at whatever they could find so that, later, they could get to a Spanish-speaking country. At the Boa Vista bus station, a young Venezuelan couple was asking, bewildered, about how far it is to Porto Alegre or Iguaçu Falls, both in the far South of Brazil. In truth, it makes no difference.

This feeling of being lost, and of trying in every possible way to give meaning to a life in transit, seems to define the immigrant experience. Ariadne, an eighteen-year-old girl from Maracay panhandling with a baby on her lap at a traffic light near Praça das Águas, a plaza in Boa Vista famous for its water fountains, says, "I went a month without eating in Venezuela; everything I got went to my grandparents." On the bus from Boa Vista and Pacaraima, Jamehary and Adrián, a mother and son, are returning to Venezuela after a two-month stint in Brazil. With them they're bringing goods, money, and food, betting that Maduro's anti-inflation policy will have an effect: "The situation in Venezuela is critical," Jamehary says. "There's nothing to eat, no clothes to wear, no medication." This back-and-forth between the two countries is constant. José María, a twenty-nine-year-old man (my age too) who sat with me during the four-hour, intoxicatingly hot ride between Pacaraima and Boa Vista, is returning to Venezuela to find his girlfriend. They were both designers in Caracas; he left the profession and came to Brazil to try his luck as a juggler, a skill he first developed as a teenage hobby. He had traveled across Brazil's northern coast, as far as the beach village of Jericoacoara, in the state of Ceará, and then convinced his girlfriend to join him.

Stories like these recur time and again. There are Venezuelans working in bars, shops, restaurants, and markets. They are asking for money on the streets, sleeping out in the open, engaging in prostitution, staying in shelters, sharing rented homes, or being temporarily "adopted" by Brazilian families.

The people of Roraima seem to understand the situation from two fundamental aspects: religion and work. And while the two don't exactly overlap, they certainly touch at several points. A welcoming spirit and the donation of goods and food are always accompanied by Christian treatises on self-sacrifice, trials and tribulations, and doing unto others. And it's the small churches that seem most active among immigrants, if not in fact at least in the view of many Roraimans and Venezuelans. The work aspect, in turn, sustains a moral filter allowing natives and immigrants alike to distinguish "decent," "hardworking," and "suffering" Venezuelans from "drifters," "criminals," and "good-for-nothing hustlers." But the world of work imposes its own contradictions, and there is a growing sense that immigrants are willing to receive less for the same labor. The "suffering worker" class is, in a way, claimed by every Venezuelan I spoke with, all of whom were attempting to distinguish themselves from the criminals. "We all pay for the actions of a few," Jamehary says, summarizing recent events in Pacaraima, as we neared the city.

I decided to meet with a number of Indigenous leaders in Roraima to talk about the hatred and prejudice they experience on a daily basis, in order to better understand the recent transference of responsibility for the state's woes, once attributed to the Indigenous people but now chalked up to the Venezuelans.

Dário Yanomami is considered one of the most important Indigenous leaders in the country. The son of Davi Kopenawa, an influential shaman and Yanomami leader, Dário is vice president of the Hutukara Yanomami Association (with his father as president), which connects and represents the various Yanomami populations and promotes their culture, publishing books about plant-based healing and their artisanal crafts. "When the Portuguese invaded our country, the prejudice was already there. It came with them. Non-Indigenous people don't deal well with us; they don't see us as people," Dário said. "As a Yanomami, I know that they (Venezuelans) are suffering, I know the prejudice."

The history of contact with the Yanomami population has drawn worldwide attention, due both to the violence of the Brazilian State and the tenacity of the Indigenous political fight. Although there had been occasional contacts since the nineteenth century, and the introduction of missionaries in the 1940s established more stable relations with the Yanomami people, it was with the developmentalism promoted by the Brazilian dictatorship during the 1970s and 1980s—road projects, settlements, farms, and the arrival of illegal gold mining—that contact became almost constant, introducing epidemics that decimated the Yanomami population. The construction of the Perimetral Norte highway (1973–1976) was key to the arrival of colonizers and prospectors who contaminated the tributaries of the Rio Branco in a true gold rush. In the early 1990s, it's been estimated that between thirty thousand and forty thousand gold miners worked the land in an area that was in the process of being recognized as the Yanomami Indigenous Territory. With a strong Indigenous political pushback, coupled with an international campaign to protect Yanomami lives and rights, the Indigenous Territory was at last demarcated in 1992 by FUNAI, drastically reducing the number of gold prospectors, though not eliminating the problem.

"We, the Yanomami, are drinking water that's full of mercury," Dário says, adding that, with the rise in gold prices in the early 2000s, prospectors reinvaded Yanomami territory with a vengeance. For him, there is a clear and direct relationship between the prospectors and politicians, especially Romero Jucá, a strong supporter of policies intended to legalize mining in Indigenous lands. "We know Jucá is funding the miners prospecting on Yanomami land, but what we don't know is who buys the gold, who the international buyers are," he notes.

Dário says he's been the target of many threats, along with his family and the entire Hutukara association. But he was chosen from among his people to fulfill this role, even though he doesn't like city life much, and returns regularly to the village to regain his strength.

He also holds the miners responsible for the murders of two isolated Yanomami people—isolated in the sense that they reject any ongoing contact with "white" society—and confirms that, with the ongoing crisis in Venezuela, many prospectors from the neighboring country are now invading their ancestral territory. According to an official statement from federal prosecutors in Roraima, a special investigation was opened in the case of the two murders, as well as a more general one with regard to mining in the region, both in civil and criminal courts. The Public Prosecutor considers this a critical moment for the Yanomami.

One fact that seems to encourage Dário is the growth of the Yanomami population, which is slowly recovering from the serious demographic losses suffered during the dictatorship. This is why he's skeptical of the white people who claim their territory is too large: nine million hectares for roughly 26,200 Indigenous people isn't much, according to Yanomami leadership, especially as the population is growing.

It's not hard to find people railing against Indigenous people in Roraima. The owner of the inn where I stayed in Boa Vista, and who adopted and looks after two twenty-year-old Venezuelan boys, doesn't hesitate to tell me that the issue of Indigenous people in Roraima is "ridiculous": "They were all imported from the Andes by Holland," he says. A driver who shuttles immigrants in shared taxis between Pacaraima and Boa Vista believes Indians are lazy, disinclined to work, and have too many lands and privileges. A miner married to an Indigenous Taurepang woman says, right next to his wife, that Indians "don't exist anymore."

Professor Braga, who is also affiliated with Insikiran Institute of Indigenous Education, a University of Roraima teaching unit focusing on Indigenous people with training in health, pedagogy, and territorial management, recalls arriving in Boa Vista for the first time, in 2005, when the city was engulfed in debate about the Raposa Serra do Sol Indigenous territory. "The day after the Supreme Court decision (which ruled that the land could only be inhabited by Indigenous people), people went out dressed in black, wearing black ribbons, mourning for Roraima," Braga says to me in his campus office. For Maria Bárbara Bethônico, also a professor at the Insikiran Institute, who specializes in the field of land management, the non-Indigenous population is quite coercive, applying pressure and arguing that the land should become more productive, in the capitalist tradition. "The discourse about the land being underutilized is quite strong," she says. "But we have to understand that it's a very different way of thinking about the land." According to Professor Bethônico, the folkloric image of the naked Indian, arrows in hand, reinforces these prejudices. Denise Wapishana, a member of the Wapishana people and a literature student, reflects on the challenges faced by Indigenous women as they move into the world of politics: "When I arrived in the city, a FUNAI employee said I had lost all my rights as an Indigenous person. But I am Wapishana regardless of whether I'm wearing white people's clothes and shoes." Denise is planning to become a bilingual teacher in her village, writing a children's book in Wapishana, and actively participating in the Indigenous political life of the city. She considers the University of Roraima campus to be "a big *maloca*," a large communal dwelling or longhouse where different Indigenous peoples can come together.

"When he finishes off the Yanomami with gold mining and disease, vengeance will fall on the head of the white man. The rivers will disappear underground, a heavy rain will destroy both the city and the jungle. This is our secret, and we will tell them," Dário says, ending the interview on a prophetic note.

The city of Pacaraima is located within the São Marcos Indigenous Territory. Once a royally owned farm, this land became private property after the 1889 Proclamation of the Republic (which overthrew Emperor Pedro II's constitutional monarchy of the Empire of Brazil), and it wasn't until 1992 that it was ratified as an Indigenous territory of the Macuxi, Taurepang, and Wapishana peoples. Unlike our usual notions of what Amazonian vegetation looks like, a series of swamps and grasslands known in both Portuguese and Spanish as "savana," defines the local landscape.

In addition to all the difficulties this city is going through with the migration crisis, there is great legal uncertainty regarding the non-Indigenous people being forced out of the Indigenous territory. Pacaraima is a small city, with around ten thousand residents, and has no capacity to generate jobs for this massive influx of immigrants. Still unable to help the Venezuelans, everyone in the municipality is showing signs of helplessness and fatigue. And the influx is increasing.

Brazilians and Venezuelan immigrants have more in common than we may imagine, considering both governments' inaction, either denying the flow of immigrants, as Maduro does, or claim to be devising action plans that never see the light of day, as then president Michel Temer's administration did. With chaos in the city streets, it took just one spark for the powder keg to explode: a well-known shopkeeper, Raimundo Nonato de Oliveira, had been assaulted and robbed, after which an ambulance—rumored to be reserved for Venezuelan immigrants only—refused to take him to the hospital in Boa Vista. In a story that would be splashed across national headlines, accompanied by some of the most disgusting, heartrending images of recent times, the local population decided to take matters into their own hands. On August 18, 2018, they attacked and expelled the immigrants, burning their belongings as they fled.

After this happened, many Brazilian residents along the border say the situation in the city has improved, though few are proud of the event or willing to admit participation. Ezequiel Matos, a driver who takes Venezuelan immigrants back and forth between Pacaraima and Boa Vista, ponders the aftermath: "If you ask the guy who threw out the Venezuelans if he thinks what he did was right. . . of course he doesn't. He burned the clothes of all these people who had nothing but the shirts on their backs." On my last day in the city, at a bar in an alley near the bus station, a group of Brazilians, both Indigenous and non-Indigenous, recounted the stories of violence they had witnessed in the city. In agonizing tones, they recalled scenes of violent expulsion, including one particular Venezuelan woman who ran off into the underbrush with garbage bags filled with clothes so she wouldn't be literally kicked out or have her belongings burned: confronted by her pleas for mercy, the attackers found themselves paralyzed. They also lamented the violence committed against the shopkeeper Raimundo Nonato, who was apparently much loved by everyone in the community.

In Santa Elena de Uairén, in Venezuela, there is massive internal migration. It is currently considered the best place in the country to live, as food can still be found there. With the new gas prices and sales controlled by the government, a complex supply system with lines stretching for kilometers has formed. Adriana Stava, a fruit vendor at a local market who is originally from Sucre, on the coast, clearly remembers the day the Brazilians expelled the Venezuelans. Buses were mobilized to assist segments of the population while others simply continued on foot: "People were still running and crying. Coming up from the border, scared to death." Adriana is considering crossing into Manaus shortly; she is frightened by the misery she sees in her native country.

In Roraima, perceptions about the arriving Venezuelans are characterized by a litany of fake news. Some say that Maduro released hundreds of prisoners who couldn't be fed in jail and dumped them at the border. A father and son who work in Boa Vista repairing refrigerators and who soon plan on returning to Caracas claim that the Venezuelans committing crimes in Brazil are the "shock troops" Maduro used to defend his government from protesters and whom he can no longer afford to pay. "They're not Venezuelans, they're Nicaraguans and Cubans with Venezuelan passports," says another, who plans to take his family to Chile and is waiting at the Pacaraima bus station for another passenger with whom he can split the costs of travel. On a local radio station, I heard a broadcaster explain that the rumor the Brazilian government would grant Venezuelans the right to vote in the next elections was false. Websites like "Roraima Sem Censura" ("Roraima Uncensored") promote a powerful mix of hate speech, inflammatory fake news, and racism against Venezuelans on a pro-Bolsonaro platform.

Using the immigration crisis for electoral gain is one of the primary sources of tension. According to a survey conducted by the Brazilian Institute of Public Opinion and Statistics, between August 13 and 16, 2018, just before Bolsonaro was stabbed in the stomach at a campaign rally, the presidential candidate was polling at 38 percent among likely voters in the state of Roraima, far outdoing his closest rival. If we ignore the null and void ballots, he could have won in the first round of voting. Bolsonaro offered the harshest rhetoric in Roraima: close the border and put an end to the state's Indigenous territories. Rhetoric that brought him a lot of attention from the non-Indigenous population, but measures that could never be implemented without violating Brazil's constitution and the international border treaties to which Brazil is a signatory. For Dário Yanomami, "If he wins the presidency, the Indians will go to war. He'll tarnish the name of Brazil and spill Indigenous blood!"

In Roraima, one of Bolsonaro's greatest allies, with highly visible billboards all across the state, is Antonio Denarium, a well-known local farmer, candidate for state government, and the man behind Frigo 10, an association of private cattle slaughterhouses in Roraima. One of the pillars of his policy proposal is agricultural development of Indigenous land and heightening security.

From what I've picked up during countless conversations, Romero Jucá is a deeply unpopular figure in Roraima. He focuses the feelings of neglect and abandonment that citizens of Roraima harbor towards the federal government. For Professor Elói Senhoras, it was Jucá's failure to take a position on the immigration crisis—as opposed to the corruption scandals and his ties to illegal mining—that destroyed his reputation. In June 2018, President Temer visited Roraima and proposed a plan for better reception of the immigrants, though very little has actually been done. In the view of the roughly one hundred thousand Venezuelans who crossed over the border, the twelve shelters in the state and the internalization process, in which a few hundred of these people were distributed across the rest of Brazil, are merely symbolic.

Perhaps one of the best examples of the government's negligence and inability to act at both the federal and state levels is the way it dealt with Venezuela's Indigenous Warao population.

These people began being removed from their traditional lands in the mid-1950s, with the agricultural boom, but it wasn't until 1980, with oil speculation sweeping across their territory in the Orinoco delta, that they were forced into migrations within Venezuela. Faced with the country's inflation crisis and lack of food, as well as mounting difficulties in obtaining grants and other aid, they came to Brazil. The Roraima government then had the idea of distributing these Indigenous people in villages throughout the region, as if this immediate action could solve the long-term problem. For Mayra Wapishana, communications director for the Indigenous Council of Roraima (CIR), "There are tremendous cultural differences and there is still a lot to discuss." The CIR has initiated a dialogue with the Warao and various social organizations to understand what actually happened to this Indigenous population in Venezuela, what they want, and how the Indigenous people of Roraima might be able to help in this situation.

As I was coming to the end of this chapter, yet another episode of hatred and violence came to pass in Boa Vista. On September 8, 2018, more than a hundred immigrants left the city after the shelter in which they were staying was attacked by Brazilians. The Brazilians murdered a Venezuelan who had killed a Brazilian who had tried to stop a small shop from being robbed. Neither the Army nor the Roraima Military Police were able to contain the attack on the temporary housing facility. It would seem that, depending on the political hay to be made from the migration crisis, the steady arrival of immigrants, and the Brazilian government's negligence, cases like this are ceasing to be so uncommon.

DONA MADALENA and her son, whose name unfortunately escapes me, own a small shop in the Cambuquira neighborhood, right on the side of the road that connects Santarém with Cuiabá, near the Nossa Senhora de Fátima school.

In this school, a few years ago, the Santarém city council set up an improvised shelter for Venezuelan refugees arriving in the city. They are mostly Indigenous Warao, from the area where the Orinoco River meets the Caribbean Sea. Although well-known and referred to casually by anyone who talks with them, this route is impressive: from the Venezuelan Caribbean on foot to Manaus, and from there by boat to Santarém. With the little they earn from handouts in the streets and small jobs in the city, these Indigenous people became accustomed to buying goods from Dona Madalena and her son.

After an inspection conducted by the Federal Public Prosecutor's office, which found the facilities at the Nossa Senhora de Fátima school to be inadequate for housing the approximately two hundred Warao who had camped out there, huddling together, the Santarém city council moved them to a new shelter. This one is located just past the Ipanema neighborhood, well down the road towards Cuiabá and within the metropolitan area. The new shelter is a farm that's prone to overheating and reached by a dirt road that runs behind a factory producing metal and cement structures.

In this new facility, to which they were relocated about two months before I went there in July 2019, the Warao complain: they only serve them chicken and rice. Every day. Just that one meal.

Whether out of habit or affection, or some other motivation, they continued returning to Cambuquira and to Dona Madalena's shop, for supplies. They convinced her and her son to open a "branch" in the trunk of their little car. Every afternoon, they load up and head out for the shelter to meet the needs of the Warao people.

I wasn't able to conduct any interviews for my story about the shelter. The Santarém city council gave me the run-around. Still, I thought it would be important to do a story, a reflection on the Warao, who, having stirred their nomadic impulses, disturb, however subtly, the rigidity of the world around them.

The Life and Death of a Minke Whale
in the Amazon

It might once have been possible to retell the history of certain peoples by the space unfamiliar animals occupied in their cultural psyches. As it was in ancient Greece, for example, where political ideas were inextricably linked with beings with half-human, half-animal characteristics. This was also true during the time of the great navigations—a foundational moment for the modern concept of Europe, and which culminated in the violent colonization of the American continents and the genocide of their native population—when Portuguese and Spanish maps were illustrated with countless imaginary creatures.

The appearance of a *Balaenoptera acutorostrata*, a minke whale, in Piquiatuba, a small village on the banks of the Tapajós River, a major tributary of the Amazon in the state of Pará, roughly a thousand kilometers from the Atlantic Ocean, aroused the imagination and curiosity not only of local people but of the entire nation, due to the case's huge media impact. Piquiatuba lies within the Tapajós National Forest, which is maintained by the ICMBio.

When it first appeared, stranded on a public beach, it was not immediately identified as a whale—an animal that was absolutely unimaginable in the middle of the Amazon. Partially covered by mud and moss, first impressions suggested it was simply a decomposing tree trunk that had been exposed during the dry season. As time went by, and with the considerable mass appearing to move at times, rumors spread that this was an animal: the great snake of the Tapajós River, perhaps; from the riverine myth about a woman who gives birth to twin snakes, which anthropologists consider to be a variant of a pre-Colombian Indigenous myth.

It was only with the arrival of Jonathás Xavier dos Santos, then a twenty-nine-year-old teacher, in a boat with his students from Piquiatuba, and their observations of water splashing from the animal's back, that the improbable conclusion was reached: the object stranded here was, in fact, a whale.

The crowded bus, with passengers and bags piled on top of one another, bounced along BR-163, the highway which connects Cuiabá, in Mato Grosso, with Santarém, in Pará. Under a scorching sun, residents were returning to their homes in the Tapajós National Forest after stopping in the city to buy bread and gallons of gas—essential purchases for those living in a place so hard to access.

It takes about three hours to travel the hundred kilometers between Santarém and Piquiatuba, which sits on the east bank of the Tapajós River, in the Belterra municipality. Piquiatuba, a reference to the towering piquia trees in the forest, was hot and muggy on the afternoon I arrived. The air felt thick without the breezes that usually help to cool the riverside communities in the late afternoon, but this was tempered by the sense of serenity and organization in the village, which has a health center, elementary school, radio, and lodging.

Remerson Castro Almeida was at the school on November 14, 2007. He was taking Jonathás Xavier dos Santos's Portuguese class when, around three in the afternoon—the hottest part of the day, some people burst into the classroom shouting, "Something's in the river spraying water like a giant caiman!" Jonathás didn't think twice; he and his class hopped in his *bajara*, a small wooden vessel commonly used in the Amazon. The whale's location was quite far from the community hub and rather difficult to access: a stream and a sand bank had to be forded in order to reach it.

At that time, the IBAMA was the administrative body responsible for the Tapajós National Forest, and they allowed cattle rearing with access to the jungle, although this is prohibited today. One of the stockbreeders asked his stepson to go after a bull that had run off to the river's edge. It was then that the young man realized the giant mass was not a decomposing tree trunk and ran back to the school. The local fishermen who first spotted the strange mass had assumed it was a fallen tree and had given it a wide berth, looking to avoid the collisions common in times of drought when the river level drops and allows large trunks to emerge, bobbing up and down in the current.

Ten minutes in the *bajara*, and the teacher and his class reached the end of the beach where the stranded animal lay. Just twelve or thirteen people in all. Cautiously, they moved around it, making sure it wasn't dangerous, considering the rumors about the great snake. Upon further examination, Jonathás verified that it was not a snake, and wondered instead if it might be a great fish, though this wasn't cause for immediate relief. Praying for the safety of his students, he moved them back to prevent them from touching the animal. Knowing that the largest fish in the region is the pirarucu, which reaches only about three meters in length, the teacher thought it could be a shark, for there are stories of such animals being caught in the area around Santarém.

It was then that Remerson, in the prime of his teenage years and endowed with a particular spirit of adolescent adventure—in his own words—took matters into his own hands and touched the animal, removing some of the silt and slime from its back. Jonathás then realized that it was a whale. Within a few hours, the place would be transformed into a veritable tourist attraction, drawing thousands of visitors in the days following the animal's discovery.

Dona Teca, Remerson's sixty-year-old mother, was born and raised in Piquiatuba. Her home, located on the river, has an open cooking area for better air circulation. Despite having many good memories of the time she lived outside the community during the 1970s, when she camped out on Ilha do Amor, one of the best-known postcard-perfect spots in all of Pará, she never quite got used to it and eventually returned to Piquiatuba.

A nostalgic if ambiguous tone dominates when she talks about the transformations Piquiatuba has undergone since she was a child: the arrival of electricity, the school, the health center, and a small supply system for groundwater are sources of pride, while changes in eating habits prompt reflections on the increase in certain diseases primarily caused by too much sugar. She remembers the time they traveled to Santarém by rowboat—a trip that took a week, even with the wind at their backs—to exchange sacks and sacks of açaí berries for candles and soap, which were then considered essentials from "outside."

The Lower Tapajós River Basin, through which the minke whale passed in 2007, is today a true battlefield, marked by confrontations between different worldviews and beliefs about the area. Development plans—which envision the construction of no fewer than forty-three hydroelectric plants across the region, and increases in deforestation as well as in mining, timber, and soybean cultivation—are just some of the threats the local population fears. These changes are an unadulterated affront to their ways of life.

Márcia Marinho Viana was a new arrival in Piquiatuba at the time of the whale's stranding. She had come to work as a teacher at the school where Sebastião dos Santos Alves Filho worked as the secretary. Today they're married, with a son and daughter, and they're afraid that the violence and disrespect being wielded against the Munduruku Indians over their land access rights, due in large part to government plans for hydroelectrical plants in the Middle Tapajós region, could have consequences for them.

In their eyes, the only reason the area they live in isn't being overrun by soybean farms, as other areas in Belterra are, is because it's a protected area, owned by the government, and therefore cannot be sold. The local community survives on fishing, hunting, and subsistence agriculture, and has recently begun investing in the creation of a community tourism agency, and also a collective of cooks, to allow resources to flow in without destroying the environmental wealth in which they live.

Despite these limited guarantees and relative stability, the greatest fear among these people is that they will eventually be physically removed from the area. Their fear is not unfounded, for the practice of removing traditional Amazonian populations has been going on since the military dictatorship began in 1964, when Indigenous people were expelled from their lands and relocated in accordance with the federal government's developmental interests. Sebastião recalls that, during the creation of the Tapajós National Forest in 1974, the inhabitants of the region had to fight to stay because the government wanted an uninhabited jungle reserve. More recently, when the Belo Monte Dam was built, countless families in the Altamira region, on the Xingu River, were forced to leave their homes, which were subsequently flooded by the hydroelectric plant.

Exhausted, agitated, with countless scrapes on its belly and a gash on its back, most likely from colliding with a boat, the minke whale needed help, which the community quickly came together to offer. On that same day, when night fell, they scheduled shifts of people to keep watch over the animal, lest it escape on its own and get lost further up the river. They also tried contacting IBAMA by phone, reporting the extraordinary case of a whale that had become stranded on one of their community's beaches and asking for help. But the body responsible for the Tapajós National Forest was skeptical. "Next time you call, why not say an elephant wandered into Piquiatuba!" was the first response. It was only when Jonathás, the educator, got on the phone that employees started believing the story and began to mobilize.

The whale appeared a week before the annual açaí festival, which draws many river residents and Indigenous visitors to Piquiatuba. As the news had already begun to spread, the day after the animal had appeared, which was a national public holiday, the community was already filling with people from other villages and communities throughout the region as well as from Santarém—which is where blogger Manuel Dutra got the scoop and broke the news to Brazil and the rest of the world.

Children scurried to take pictures next to and on top of the whale while community members took turns covering it with damp sheets to protect it from sunburn. This remote region, about a kilometer from the center of Piquiatuba, had become one massive parking lot. Four-by-four trucks, with enough power to ford the river and cross the sandbar that separate the beach where the animal lay from the path that leads to the village, parked very close to the stranding site. Smaller cars pulled over at the water's edge, and their occupants continued on foot up to the whale.

Throughout the day, biologists and veterinarians from IBAMA and the Santarém city council arrived on site and initiated appropriate veterinary treatments. Meanwhile, IBAMA contacted the Instituto Baleia Jubarte, or Humpback Whale Institute, which immediately dispatched Milton Marcondes, a veterinarian responsible for monitoring the breeding of humpbacks in the Atlantic Ocean off the coast of Bahia state. But despite the best efforts of the community, the whale managed to escape that night.

The end of the beach where the whale was stranded is a muddy area of the Tapajós riverbank, full of *cauxi*, a type of stinging freshwater sponge that remains on the banks when the water level drops during the dry season. On the sandy part of the beach, Remerson and Sebastião point to myriad scattered pieces of Indigenous pottery: ceramics of different shapes, colors, sizes, and materials which community members identify as belonging to their Indigenous ancestors, and which still lack in-depth archaeological studies, making this location something of a huge, abandoned cemetery.

Although they don't consider themselves Indigenous, the population of Piquiatuba speaks respectfully of its ancestors and seems to have much admiration for its neighbors in Takuara and Bragança, which were among the first communities in the Lower Tapajós River Basin to identify themselves as Indigenous at the end of the twentieth century. This process is locally acknowledged as a time of reorganization for the Indigenous movement, in which the population begins to recognize and claim their rights, living in villages and questioning the violent narrative of the whitening process in the name of appreciation and validation for their ways of life.

It takes a little under two hours by boat to get from Piquiatuba, on the east bank of the Tapajós, to the Tupinambá villages of Jaguarituba and Santo Amaro, on the west bank of the Tapajós-Arapiuns Extractive Reserve. It's a frightening crossing, and many local residents wished us good luck and to take care, as we were going out in a small vessel with a tiny outboard motor into the turbulence of this immense river.

From what the locals say—and everyone seems to know even the most peculiar details of this story—after escaping from Piquiatuba, the whale went unseen for several long hours before becoming stranded again the next day, November 16, on a beach between Jaguarituba and Santo Amaro. Inhabitants of both villages had heard about the whale, and were preparing to cross the river to see the animal when they learned it had escaped. So it came as a surprise to the Indigenous people when local fishermen announced that the animal had come to a stop right there, between the two villages.

Despite the whale's being well cared-for as well as enjoyed—as attested by the many photos taken of adults by its side and children climbing on its back—the animal escaped again. But this time, there was an additional, important detail: a rumor that the whale had been wounded by a harpoon or arrow during its stay in Jaguarituba and Santo Amaro. Some even said it was beaten with a stick and killed. These stories stigmatized the two communities as places where the whale was harmed.

Such speculations are quickly countered by the local Indigenous people, who claim that the animal already had a deep wound in its back, an observation also made by residents of Piquiatuba and by Jonathás, the teacher, and later corroborated by a veterinary report which states the likely cause of the gash was a collision with a boat. In addition, Seu Azulai, a Jaguarituba resident, looked under the fins and reported seeing several *candiru*—a kind of fish known as a bloodsucker. "We were very sorry, because we took very good care of her," he said, showing us photos of the event from his collection and inviting us to take a bath in the stream that runs underneath his house.

While unusual, it is not unprecedented to find a whale swimming into a river. In 2006, a northern bottlenose whale, a species that can grow up to five meters long and seven metric tons in weight, ran aground in the River Thames in central London. It had gone off-course from the icy seas of Scotland and Northern Ireland as it was departing the Arctic Ocean in search of less frigid waters. It was the first whale seen in London since records began in 1913. And in November 2016, a humpback whale, which can weigh up to thirty metric tons and reach sixteen meters in length, was seen in New York's Hudson River near the George Washington Bridge. She didn't run aground, and was likely able to find her way back to salt water. In fact, American scientists have recorded an increase in whale sightings in the New York Area over the past several years. They credit this to better water quality and increasing populations of Atlantic menhaden, a favorite prey of humpbacks. These improvements in environmental conditions is likely the result of public policies passed back in the 1970s.

The minke whale in the Tapajós River, in turn, broke all records, and is considered the cetacean (an infraorder of marine animals which includes whales) that has traveled the longest distance upstream: more than a thousand kilometers from Marajó Island, in the Amazon River Delta, where it entered, to the beach in Piquiatuba.

Also known around the world as the *zwergal* (German for "dwarf whale") and the *vågehval* (Norwegian for "bay whale"), the minke belongs to the Mysticeti suborder, characterized by having baleen: structures more like bristles in the mouth instead of teeth. In order to feed, these animals draw in huge volumes of water and filter out the plankton or krill, a group of invertebrates similar to shrimp. This particular species usually spends the summers feeding in Antarctica before heading north for warmer waters during the winter. In November, then, with the austral summer approaching, this particular minke would have been making its way back to Antarctica on an empty stomach when, for some reason, it entered the mouth of the Amazon River.

It was in the midst of a heated game of pool, on the eve of the November 15 holiday, at a bar in Caravelas, in southern Bahia, that Milton Marcondes received an unusual call from Fábia Luna, at IBAMA, with whom he had previously worked. After taking the call, Milton told his friends that he had to leave immediately on an emergency trip. The mission? To rescue a whale in the middle of the Amazon. His friends didn't buy it, believing Milton was just changing the subject as a lame excuse for abandoning the game.

Marcondes spent the entire night and much of the next day traveling. He went from Caravelas to Vitória, and from there to Rio, Brasília, and Manaus before finally arriving in Santarém. For two days, November 16 and 17, Marcondes joined team searching for the animal by helicopter, without any real hope of finding it, when the next day they got a report that the whale had reappeared at the mouth of the Arapiuns River in São José do Arapixuna, just northwest of Santarém.

The whale had been found stranded near the shore. Again, it had been covered with damp cloths to protect it from the sun, and Marcondes put together a first aid plan: dive underwater to check for injuries, take the necessary measures, and hold tight until a large net arrived from Santarém which they would use to contain the animal in a nearby tributary while providing for its recovery.

When the net failed to arrive, Milton began his work, though observing the animal from underwater proved difficult due to the murky water. He felt around with his hands, and confirmed the presence of a superficial wound, which locals assumed had been caused by an arrow or stick. Pink river dolphins appeared around the whale, as if offering their support to their suffering distant cousin. Milton treated the animal with antibiotics and was preparing to perform blood tests when the rescue helicopter landed again. The whale started to tremble: it looked like it might be a seizure, but Milton soon realized the animal was frightened by the noise and rotor wash from the helicopter's arrival.

Panicked, the animal escaped again, and began swimming in circles. By then it was late in the afternoon, and the lack of light made a safe capture risky for both the animal, which could get caught up in the newly arrived netting and drown, and for the people attempting to rescue it, who could easily be crushed by its seven-ton mass. Considering such dangers, the decision was made to postpone the operation to the next day. Around ten o'clock that night, the people along the riverbank monitoring the whale could no longer hear its breathing. The next morning, the animal was gone, and nowhere to be found.

Searches were resumed, but in vain. The whale would only reappear on November 20, on the same beach from which it had disappeared two days before, its carcass distended and already in a state of advanced decomposition—a detail that truly astonished the veterinarian.

Raimundo Castro das Neves, now an evangelical minister, was forty at the time of the minke whale's stranding, and living between Piquiatuba and Alter do Chão along a route he still takes every week to work with relatives in the tourist village's burgeoning construction industry. He recalls with excitement how he boarded the helicopter sent by IBAMA to search for the whale on the night of November 15, when it escaped from Piquiatuba. But they were never able to spot it. Convinced that the whale's fate could have been different, Raimundo deeply regrets that the Piquiatuba community wasn't able to resolve the issue on its own. He admits that he cried when he first learned of the animal's death.

Among the other possibilities suggested by community members was situating the whale between two catamarans and sailing the thousand kilometers separating Piquiatuba from the sea, thus returning the whale to the open Atlantic Ocean. The human and financial costs of such an undertaking, however, were prohibitive. The other plan they had discussed was to gather a group of strong men to carry the whale, in their arms, to the large lake in the heart of Piquiatuba. Packed with fish, they believed there would have been plenty of food for the whale to happily live out its life with them.

Owing to the cetacean's arrival, Piquiatuba gained fame as "the place where the whale appeared." Everyone in the region knows the story, everyone enjoys retelling it, and many, to my surprise, were quick to remember that 2017 was its tenth anniversary. The beachings were a landmark event for the community, and the subject of countless projects and activities by students in the local schools—in addition to the basic curriculum these schools run classes on Amazonian Studies and the History of Belterra.

Sávio Viana Alves, Sebastião and Márcia's son, wasn't even born when the minke whale appeared in Amazonian waters. Even so, he is well aware of what happened. "If it were me, I wouldn't have let the whale die. I would have dug a well for her to stay in," the six-year-old says. I also had the opportunity to talk with an elementary school class whose students at the time of the whale's appearance would have been only two or three years old, yet this does not limit their affection for the story. "I would have liked her a lot," "I'd give her a hug," and "I'd take a selfie" were some of the students' statements about how they would react if another whale were to appear in their community.

Some of the activities organized by the school to respond to the event were storytelling and holding discussions about it, as well as artwork—all of which was lost when one of the school's computers died during a storm.

One of the most striking passages in Herman Melville's *Moby-Dick* is the moment when the narrator and protagonist, Ishmael, reflects on the importance of whales to contemporary commerce in its global form. He implies that, despite the insignificance of whaling in world literature and the low status that whalers occupy in nineteenth-century American society, it is precisely they who are primarily responsible for the growing geopolitical importance of the United States. This was happening, according to Ishmael, because only whaling, and the commercialization of whale oil for lighting, had managed to break the Spanish stranglehold on trade in the Pacific between its Asian and American colonies and the motherland:

> Until the whale fishery rounded Cape Horn, no commerce but colonial, scarcely any intercourse but colonial, was carried on between Europe and the long line of the opulent Spanish provinces on the Pacific coast. It was the whalemen

who first broke through the jealous policy of the Spanish crown, touching those colonies; and, if space permitted, it might be distinctly shown how from those whalemen at last eventuated the liberation of Peru, Chili, and Bolivia from the yoke of Old Spain, and the establishment of the eternal democracy in those parts.

One of the subsequent stages in the development of modern international trade was tied directly to the creation of Belterra. In 1934, the industrialist Henry Ford decided to clear the jungle and create a rubber plantation for latex extraction, eventually intended to supply the tires of his cars, which sold around the world. Belterra was designed and built as a village for American workers, complete with hospitals, schools, basic sanitation, and a brand-new port to handle the rubber production. The residents of Piquiatuba, in turn, took advantage of the new demand and began extracting latex from rubber trees themselves, which they went on to sell in Belterra.

Ultimately, it is no exaggeration to say that the current arrangement of international trade has one of its geopolitical nodes right there in the Lower Tapajós region: as much due to the soy produced in Mato Grosso (and already spreading across Pará), which helps sustain growth in China, as to the potential for deforestation to establish new, clear acreage coveted by factory farms.

The João Fona Cultural Center, whose façade looks out over the Tapajós River in downtown Santarém, has an impressive collection of Amazonian archaeology, as well as displays featuring historic documents and furniture from the city, a temporary exhibition room, and our whale's skeleton on display: the most visited attraction by far. The building, built in 1865, has previously served as the city hall, the Santarém Chamber of Commerce, the courthouse, and the jail.

Jussara Silva de Almeida, an educator responsible for the institution's library and for leading some of the guided tours, seems excited about the way things are going at the cultural center, which is currently partnering a teaching and knowledge creation program not only with local schools but with the greater Santarém community and tourists as well. Many visitors, especially the locals and their children, come just to see the whale. Tourists who are unaware of the story often assume the bones have been brought there for some other reason.

Even so, the João Fona staff are not short of stories to tell. For example, there was the teacher who, upon entering the exhibition room, was struck by the size of the bones: "A dinosaur!" she exclaimed. And then there are the old fishermen from the region, who enjoy comparing this animal to the large fish and caimans they caught when they were young.

But the story that most appeals to Jussara—and she's heard it several times—has to do with the whale's supposed route into Amazonian waters: according to some, foreign ships would arrive, loaded with salt water from the ocean, which was then emptied into the river so they could then steal clean fresh water from the region. During one of these operations, the whale must have been dumped in the Tapajós, and, unable to find its way back to the Atlantic, ended up stranded in Piquiatuba.

The likelihood of such a tale is irrelevant. In a more or less imaginary sense, its value lies in its being one of the ways the local population reflects on life and the political issues of their time. It is a poetic conception, a way of giving meaning to the world as it transforms around them, even stemming as it does from an event as unusual and peculiar as the life and death of a minke whale in the Amazon.

An Afternoon with Venezuelans at the Manaus Bus Terminal Overpass

"The war of liberation goes on. Like during the colonial days, with the Indigenous people and *criollos* fighting over turf." This remark, at once sad and playful, made by Aníbal Gutierrez, a Venezuelan immigrant, refers to the daily conflicts in the camp where the Venezuelans live beneath an overpass near the Manaus Bus Terminal, in the south-central part of the capital of Amazonas state.

On March 18, 2019, a hot Monday afternoon, the usual insults and tensions reached their peak and then boiled over into violence. Stones and pieces of lumber flew over the tents pitched precariously on the grass next to the bus station where Indigenous and non-Indigenous Venezuelans sleep on the ground, under long haul trucking tarps or on worn-out mattresses. They threatened one another with machetes, fishing knives, and kitchen knives. Women and children ran off, scared, while the men squared off. Some were courageous enough to get between the factions and try to separate them. A rock hit Ana Cuparis in the belly. Just a few moments earlier, right when we had started our interview, I had explained that I wanted to know the story of her life. Simply, dryly, and with downcast eyes, she replied: "It's a sad one."

Ana's ribs were badly bruised, but she's doing well. At least, as well as someone living in such conditions can be. The next day, she went back to her routine, asking for food at intersections, one of her three children on her hip, while her husband, Andrés Perez, either takes care of the other two or does small jobs as a painter, taking care of cars in the street, or weeding some land. The money he earns from painting, weeding, or "whatever," as Andrés says, goes to support not only the five members of his migrant family but also his parents back in Venezuela.

This story's protagonists had already been determined long before all this started, although they don't seem to have much control over the script in which their lives are playing out and which brought them to this bleak state of affairs. Aníbal Gutierrez was a food vendor: "There are no living conditions in Venezuela," he says. Marco Garcia was a lawyer: "I'm not used to this type of life." Ravel Ribero is one of the leaders of the Warao Indigenous people at the camp: "The *criollos* are killing us," he says. "They call us Indians; they threaten and bully us." A Brazilian panhandler, most likely drunk, calls out to a passing officer: "Our president has to get them out of here. That's why we voted for Bolsonaro, we're going to be in charge." Sergeant Gonçalves, one of the beat cops assigned to the bus terminal area, comments: "While the government agencies are dragging their feet and looking the other way, it all falls on the shoulders of the police." He goes on: "It's like we're beating a dead horse. . . . We look incompetent because we're dealing with a problem that's not ours to fix."

That same afternoon, in Washington, President Jair Bolsonaro, was praising the United States' military power in a speech on resolving the crisis in Venezuela. Back at the camp riven with internal conflicts, the news went unnoticed.

In Brazil, depending on how it's used, the Spanish term *criollo*, meaning "creole," can have negative connotations. In Venezuela, however, it's simply the way the non-Indigenous population understands itself as Venezuelan: a mixed population of Indigenous, African, and European descent. The theory of miscegenation, of being creole, is one supported by the Venezuelan elite as a foundation of their national identity, of how people become Venezuelan. In a way, this tension is being reproduced on Brazilian soil in a tiny space next to the Manaus Bus Terminal which some three hundred people now call home. The clash between Indigenous and non-Indigenous people that took place that afternoon harkens back to a conflict over land that eventually formed the nation of Venezuela itself, along with so many other Latin American countries.

The situation at the camp is extremely precarious, and basic hygiene for the dozens of families that share the cramped space is practically nonexistent. During the Amazonian rainy season, a considerable part of the day revolves around trying to keep themselves—and their very few possessions—dry. Tuberculosis and pneumonia are two of the primary illnesses that affect Venezuelan migrants in Brazil.

The kitchen is a communal one, utilizing improvised wood stoves, or larger ones donated by evangelical churches. Frozen chickens in the process of defrosting share space with yucca in pots set out on the floor where people pass by and children play. The bus station bathroom attendant, who is in charge of collecting restroom fees—one Brazilian *real*, or approximately seventeen cents—says "When you can't pay, I'll let you in. What else can you do?"

The experience of exile is characterized by the loss of references, and by a great difficulty in getting around, in understanding and in attributing some semblance of meaning to what has happened in each person's life. Loss of references is, perhaps, an overly elegant term for "confusion." Confusion at facing a new language, a new territory, another bureaucratic system to deal with. The Indigenous Warao, who are skilled fishermen in the area where the Orinoco River meets the Atlantic Ocean, don't see how are they supposed to fish in Amazonian waters. How are they, who struggle to communicate in Spanish, to know where the fish are, which way the currents and eddies run, or how the boats and ships navigate the rivers around a major city like Manaus?

This confusion is widespread. Understanding the bureaucratic nature of the Brazilian State is a challenge for anyone. Decipher me or I'll devour you, it seems to say. And many do end up devoured. Upon arriving in Pacaraima, on Roraima's border with Venezuela, Venezuelans are met by Brazilian immigration agents and assisted by UNHCR, the United Nations agency that assists refugees. At this point, they are documented and submit a request for asylum, which grants them a "CPF," which is their individual tax identification number, as well as a vaccination card and a work permit. But each of these procedures has its own complicated maze of forms, payments, mailings, requests, and internet access requirements. With long lines, delays, and frequent crashes in Pacaraima's local registration system, "people get frustrated and end up just going to whatever city they're heading for without getting the proper documentation," says Aníbal. To him, Brazil is a rich country, a great producer of cereals and other foods, but "it wasn't prepared for this wave of people."

The Warao were the first residents of the camp established behind the Manaus International Bus Terminal in early 2017, when migration to the Amazon capital began to intensify (the first groups began arriving in late 2016). They were later removed from the site and instead put up in houses and sheds, but they still return regularly to the Orinoco River Delta to bring food and medical supplies to relatives who stayed in the neighboring country. The money they're able to raise comes from both donations and selling craftwork. Along the way, in Roraima, between 2014 and 2016, many of these Venezuelans were arrested and deported by the Brazilian Federal Police, provoking strong reactions from international human rights organizations. Today, many can be found in cities like Santarém and Belém in the state of Pará.

In the camp beneath the overpass, most of the conversations revolve around the search for work and the challenges of earning a livelihood. In Venezuela, Aníbal worked as a self-employed vendor in the food industry. With the astronomical inflation, he went bankrupt, no longer having clientele with whom to conduct business. "Before, prices were adjusted daily," he said. "Then it was every hour." He continues, "Since we can't find jobs, we can't afford a place to rent. So we came here, to the overpass near the bus station. To survive." He complains vociferously about what he sees as a game of economic interests with regard to immigrants: "International organizations like Caritas and the UNHCR see us as nothing but capital. Each new Venezuelan means more money in their budgets," says Aníbal, who, along with several others, is building a reception center for immigrants, and which he proposes will be run by the immigrants themselves.

"The love that Brazilians have for Venezuelans, the kindness that Brazilians have for Venezuelans. . . . They welcomed us with such hospitality. Thanks to all of this, we're surviving," Aníbal Gutierrez declares. But as he talks graciously of Brazilian courtesy, my thoughts drift away, revisiting everything I have witnessed earlier that afternoon. I'm thinking, in particular, of what Aníbal and his camp colleagues might have said if the Brazilian government had, in fact, orchestrated a welcoming committee worthy of human beings.

Indigenous Warao and non-Indigenous Venezuelans disagree about what exactly caused the conflict that Monday afternoon. According to Ravel Ribero, the Warao *cacique*, "They were stealing money straight out of a (Warao) girl's hand." But Aníbal claims a young man "found fifty *reais* on the ground, and the Indigenous people said the money was theirs." It's impossible to know the truth, and in this situation, it may not even matter. The Warao and the Venezuelan *criollos* live as best they can, seeking refuge despite its difficulties, despite being neglected by both the Brazilian government, which refuses to accept them, and the Venezuelan government, which denies the immigration crisis altogether. They are characters in a story they'd rather not be writing. "If the crisis in Venezuela hadn't happened, we wouldn't be here," says Ravel. "In Venezuela, we'd already be dead."

AT THE MANAUS BUS TERMINAL, trying to get close enough to interview the Venezuelans living beneath the nearby overpass, I found myself caught up in a situation that might not have ended very well. Shortly after arriving at the camp, I was directed by the immigrants to something of an improvised living room comprised of old sofas and other furniture in an advanced state of disrepair, where the refugees were able to protect themselves from both the sun and the rain, and to keep what meager belongings they were carrying with them.

I can't even remember if I had gotten past the very uncomfortable point of introducing myself and explaining the story I wanted to write when I felt a hand tugging my wallet out of my back pocket. I was afraid to make any sudden moves. Not knowing quite what to do, and hoping to avoid any sort of conflict—I had barely arrived—I simply repositioned my hand near my hip. The stranger's fingers withdrew from my pocket. I continued the truncated conversation with the residents about my objectives there without ever learning whose hand had been in my pocket. I was explaining how I wanted to report on the situation they had found themselves in when I felt the hand approaching again. The whole thing was tricky, and I was extremely tense.

I decided to try and diffuse the whole situation, saying it wasn't cool that they were trying to rob me. One of the young men who was sitting nearby intensified his gaze and began cleaning his nails with a machete. He didn't say a word, nor otherwise imply he might make a move. His look was disapproving and threatening enough.

I said if it went on like this, I'd drop the idea and leave them alone. The hand which until than I had only sensed near my butt, and which I had avoided looking directly at, suddenly revealed itself as that of a grinning youngster with a rascally laugh, as if to say "chill out," that everything was just a joke.

I decided to utilize what assets I had. I told them that, as a journalist, I had made a commitment to be ethical, that I sympathized with their situation, and that they should take a moment to think about whether or not they might want something published that would expose the conditions they were living in, camped out under the bridge.

I said I'd leave calmly, no hard feelings, but a report—however brief, however few its readers—could improve their situation, at least to some small degree. It might even generate enough attention to stir up some government aid or donations from the people of Manaus, made aware of the difficulties experienced by hundreds of Venezuelan families sheltering beneath an overpass.

"*Has hablado bien*," came a voice from among them. "You've spoken well." The small crowd that had surrounded me began to disperse. The mistrustful-looking young man finished cleaning his nails, set his machete aside, and we began talking.

The Self-Demarcation of Tupinambá Indigenous Land in the Lower Tapajós River Basin

"Hey, Fábio . . . imagine all this here turning into soy." With a somewhat apprehensive smile and an uneasy look in his eyes, this comment by Seu Braz, *cacique* of the Tupinambá in the Lower Tapajós River Basin, on the first day of an intense hike through the rainforest, was a sincere declaration about the dangers to the region. The Indigenous leader, whose village of São Francisco lies within the Tapajós-Arapiuns Extractive Reserve, in Santarém, state of Pará, organized with other Tupinambá warriors and began to open up a trail, independently demarcating their ancient territory, for many reasons. On the one hand, there are the growing threats from the expansion of agricultural, timber, and mining corporations; on the other, there is the failure of FUNAI, Brazil's National Indian Foundation, to take action, and the federal government's unwillingness to protect the rights of Indigenous peoples.

For ten days I accompanied the Indigenous organization as it moved through the region and into the rainforest, beginning the process of marking their territories' boundaries. Over five of those days, we hiked roughly forty kilometers through the jungle, carving out a trail that rarely exceeded two meters in width. While the formal interviews with the Tupinambá warriors, as they're known, were valuable, it was only during the daily marches, as we shared in the efforts and challenges of the jungle, that I became aware of the extent of the political struggle in which they were locked.

Established between the late 1990s and the early 2000s, the Tapajós-Arapiuns Extractive Reserve, which covers over 677,000 hectares, came to include several Indigenous territories whose people were engaged in an intense struggle over their rights. The process was seen as a reorganization of the Indigenous movement in the region, a movement which fought for the reserve's very constitution, considering it a way of defending their lands and ways of life. Nearly twenty years later, however, the reality on the ground—marked by the growing power of the Indigenous movement and the rejection of repeated proposals for damaging clear-cutting, strip mining, and other extractive uses of the land, some of which are being mediated by the ICMBio—has sparked a struggle for the establishment of a unified Indigenous Territory where the extractive reserve lies today.

Threats made against the region and its people are deeply woven into the stories of those who share this territory. Many of those who took to the forest to protect their land once worked for the Santa Isabel lumber company, which was forced out by the establishment of the extractive reserve. According to the Indigenous community, the company's objective was complete deforestation in preparation for massive fields of soy: they illegally removed *ipês* and *mandioqueiras* and resold them in Europe with a green sustainability label. For Seu Ezeriel and his wife the *cacica* Estevina, from the village of Cabeceira do Amorim (where they and their whole family are staunch supporters of self-demarcation), the open fields and pastures Ezeriel had seen in Amapá, where he had traveled a few years before, appeared to predict the future for the land where he had been born, were it not for the establishment of the extractive reserve and the expulsion of the lumber company.

The fact is, during the nearly two decades the reserve has been in existence, plenty of other threats to the local Indigenous and riverine populations have emerged. ICMBio has been promoting a number of projects that endanger their ways of life, which is defined by an intimate relationship with the rainforest, both with regard to the abundance of fishing and hunting options, as well as access to water and medicinal techniques that come from an age-old understanding of the jungle. Recently, a number of riverine villages and other communities got together to debate and put a stop to two interconnected proposals: one that would effectively have put a price tag on the forest by implementing a carbon credit program under which Finland would own the land, and a second that would have managed and harvested the lumber.

The Indigenous population rejected these proposals. They were concerned about establishing a carbon credit program at the extractive reserve, which would incur a fee whenever a tree was cut down to build a canoe or to create a swidden, thus reversing the relationship between ownership and custody of the region. In effect, their very lifestyle would, under the carbon credit program, be considered a form of deforestation. Such a proposal would have limited the access of people in the Tapajós-Arapiuns Extractive Reserve to the natural resources necessary for their existence. In a powerfully mobilized demonstration, scores of Indigenous people occupied ICMBio in Santarém and managed to suspend the project.

As we cleared our trail, sustaining ourselves primarily on manioc flour and game from the rainforest, we were careful to make sure that self-demarcation wouldn't "invade" the territory of other Indigenous peoples. Even though the creation of one common Indigenous Territory was discussed a number of times, the Tupinambá had decided to take matters into their own hands, hoping to put pressure on the government and force it to recognize the area as their own Indigenous land, thus encouraging other villages to follow suit and bolstering the hopes of a unified Indigenous Territory in the area currently occupied by the reserve.

Anthropologists and scholars are aware of the sociopolitical phenomenon that is the reorganization of the Indigenous movement in the Lower Tapajós River Basin and the Arapiuns River. Seu Braz categorically refuses to use the term "emerging Indians," often used of populations who have recently demanded that their condition as Indigenous be officially affirmed. "We have always been Indians," he says. Other testimony, such as that of Dona Nazaré, an eighty-seven-year-old who has lived her entire life in Cabeceira do Amorim, points to the violent processes of colonization and eradication of identity that many have experienced. Like her daughter, the *cacica* Estevina, Dona Nazaré has established a dynamic connection between Indigenous past, the violence they experienced, and the Indigenous future, situated as it is in the midst of their current political struggles and demands for education specifically designed to rekindle traditions for younger generations.

Still, though, plenty of politicians and businessmen, and a significant part of the judicial system, insist that there are no Indigenous people remaining in the region, as if cultural identity and ways of life could simply be erased by colonial violence, as if the Indigenous peoples were unable to reinvent themselves as a power critically opposed to the process being imposed upon them. The proposal of a unified Indigenous Territory in the extractive reserve, one respecting the region's other inhabitants, is one of the primary topics to be discussed by the movement this year. One of the crucial issues is that of negotiating with the residents of other communities and villages who do not consider themselves Indigenous. For the Tupinambá, though, the fight to defend the territory is a fight for all, because if the rainforest is cut down, or a carbon credit market established, the negative effects on hunting and water supplies will affect all residents, Indigenous and non-Indigenous alike. Therefore, self-demarcation is closely tied to what many Tupinambá see as a way of being Indigenous and to the rejection of a way of life in which urban work and the buying and selling of goods are central. It is an act of political resistance amid a constant state of war.

My personal involvement in the early phases of this self-demarcation was a condition set by the Indigenous people themselves: I was tasked with using GPS technology to help mark the boundaries of the Tupinambá's territory and guide the hike through the dense rainforest. With a profound understanding of the forest and the ability to guide themselves by the movements of the clouds, the Tupinambá warriors soon demonstrated that the GPS was merely a secondary tool in the process. As for myself and Dani (a graphic artist who also participated in the hike, holding drawing workshops with the children), we ended up needing help rather than actually contributing.

The relationship with the land and the protection of a way of life are the two salient elements in this political struggle. Fundamental to Indigenous cosmology, the Enchanters and Protectors of Waters and Forests seem to be taking part in the fight against the new ways their territory is being exploited. The Mãe d'Água ("Water Mother"), the Mãe da Mata ("Forest Mother"), and other forest beings are woven into the fabric of the Indigenous people's concerns about the political conflict in the region and the greater world around them. They surface in stories like the one told by Seu Edno, the night before they set off to mark their borders, of a man who mistreated animals until, in a dream, he saw himself transfigured into a peccary and hunted. Stories like this can be considered a perfect equivalent to many Amerindian myths. Particularly striking is the belief in a lake where the elders went fishing and left with only a small catch of manatees, leaving the rest to the Enchanted Beings. This lake has long since disappeared, and yet could resurface, unleashing fresh forces. According to some, this same lake could help to confound the technology used by Petrobras, the state-owned oil company, to detect underground oil reserves.

Self-demarcation is the struggle for this land, for the right to manage it according to the Tupinambá's own rules and requirements; for a particular way of life, in which a relationship with the rainforest and the Enchanted Beings is of the utmost importance; for a way of life that runs contrary to the impositions of other cultures, in which financial trade and commerce are so central. After expressing his concerns that his territory would face the same fate as the deforested land and open fields he saw Amapá, Seu Ezeriel told a joke of no small consequence—and I will end this story with it:

There was a doctor on a boat. He asked the mestizo boatman:

"Can you read, copperskin?"

"Well, no . . ."

"So you've wasted half your life," said the doctor.

After a few more strokes, the copper-skinned boatman asks:

"Doctor, do you know how to swim?"

"Absolutely not!"

"Then you've wasted your entire life," replied the boatman.

CHUMBO   PÓLVORA   ESPOLETA   BUCHA

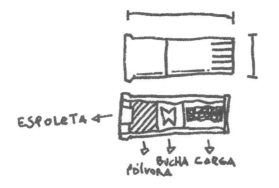

ESPOLETA →

PÓLVORA   BUCHA   CARGA

WHILE ORGANIZING MY RETURN to a Tupinambá village in Pará, the locals suggested I buy some canvas tarpaulins, provisions, and shotgun shells. We were getting ready to spend a week in the rainforest.

I had very little skill with or knowledge of firearms. The closest I ever came to firing one was when I passed a rifle from one hunter to another, in the middle of the jungle in the dead of night, afraid that it would go off on its own.

I was dreading going shopping for ammunition in Santarém. I was advised to focus my efforts on the Tapajós riverfront around Mercadão 2000, the large open-air market.

At every shop and storefront, every person I asked for help responded with a quick, suspicious look followed by a brusque "no." After three or four attempts, I finally realized they thought I was a police officer. Standing roughly six feet tall and dressed in sports gear, I doubt anybody could have confused me with an unlicensed Indigenous hunter looking to buy ammunition.

Frustrated and afraid of disappointing the waiting crew, I was on the point of giving up when I decided to try one more store: the grimiest, most chaotic one yet. I asked for ammo. The owner gave me the same suspicious look that greeted me whenever I asked this question. Expecting to be denied once again and forced to abandon my mission for good, I was then asked, "Is it for you?"

This was the first time someone had answered me with another question.

"Yes," I stammered. "For me, and for the people I'll be hunting with," I quickly added.

"So you hunt?" he countered again.

I got the feeling this conversation wasn't going to last much longer under that withering gaze, so I decided to be as open and honest as possible: "I just go along with the hunters. I'm a researcher, actually."

"What, biology?" the shopkeeper asked, his expression unchanged.

The conversation had finally turned in my favor, and I didn't want to risk that with a lie. "I study people's relationships with the rainforest," I summarized.

That seemed to satisfy him. As for myself, I was relieved. My beard might have persuaded him that I wasn't an undercover cop, though I could tell he wasn't completely convinced. He sent a young helper to measure out the shot. Not having to perform that function, he could keep his eyes on me. I didn't want to make any wrong moves: playing with my cell phone would have been the worst idea of all, for he would likely assume I was either calling in backup officers to catch him in the act, or photographing and recording the scene. I chose—or pretended—to entertain myself by looking at the spare parts and tools for the boat engines he was selling.

I was quite relieved, assuming the transaction was going well, when the shopkeeper started asking questions again: "Which caliber? How many grams of powder?" I had no idea how to respond. Instead, I was happy to accept his recommendations, which I'm sure by that point had fully exposed me as someone who had never fired a shot in his life.

I vaguely remembered that there was something else I was supposed to buy other than the shells, but the exact word eluded me. Having made it through the initial trial by fire, I took a chance: "Do you sell shotguns too?"

"No!" the shopkeeper spat, in the same tone I had heard time and again that morning. He completed the sale and shooed me out of his store.

It was only after I had returned to the village, and attempted to explain why I hadn't brought the full list of purchases, that I understood my mistake: I had confused *escopeta*, a shotgun, with *espoleta*, the primer. Without that, the weapons wouldn't fire.

My Tupinambá hosts spent most of the next week jeering and joking with me over this story.

Anamã:
Six Months Underwater,
Six Months on Dry Land

Between the two extremes of floods and droughts that come with the Solimões stretch of the Amazon River, the town of Anamã has already seen the hospital submerged and the local cemetery relocated twice.

In Anamã, most problems begin and end with water. The town is located deep in the heart of the rainforest, and so the people there are well supplied with fish while still able to pursue small-scale agricultural production. Floods, which can last more than five months, force them to adapt everything, from their own habits to the town's very architecture. During the dry season, the water grows muddy, the fish die, and access to the large nearby lake and other rural communities becomes all but impossible. Most of the time, water for human consumption is very poor quality: turbid, ferrous, and rank. Here, global warming is not some far-flung hypothesis, whose effects will only be felt in the distant future, but a daily reality.

Starting in mid-December, when an increase in rainfall raises the levels of the Amazon and Purus rivers, Anamã goes underwater. The flooding can last through the month of June. As there's no sewage system, when the water rises, the home-made outhouses start to overflow. Being on a floodplain, the soil is already saturated, and therefore unable to absorb additional inundations. There's a spike in snake bites and scorpion stings, as animals begin looking for floating structures as refuge. Caimans invade backyards and gardens.

This is also when outbreaks of diarrhea, fungal infections, and Hepatitis A and B start to occur. Even when people walk through streets that aren't entirely flooded, the standing water is dirty and contaminated by the fecal coliform bacteria from the outhouses. This is water that drains at an achingly slow rate.

As the waters rise, the river's flow increases, and human waste and other effluvia are washed away by the current. The water power is weakened by floating houses along the banks of this tiny tributary of the Amazon that work like a sieve, regulating the flow and preventing large tree trunks from entering the town. All vehicles have to be taken by ferry to the town of Manacapuru, ninety kilometers away, and local transportation is done exclusively by canoes and launches. Getting to school or church, policing, garbage collection, shopping, going to bars near the main square . . . every aspect of life and death involves boats and water.

Motorcycle taxis stop operating—they have yet to develop a canoe-taxi system—and the drivers have to take on other roles, such as fisherman and dockhand, the latter being somewhat less strenuous than otherwise as the high water means it's no longer necessary to trudge up and down the steep ramp to the river terminal. Some fishermen claim the floods bring greater hauls, but others don't feel this to be entirely true. There is definitely a drop in commerce, and all agricultural production of manioc, yams, bananas, and watermelons, which are cultivated in the rural areas surrounding the community and usually sold in markets in Anamã and Manaus, is lost.

Periods of flooding and drought are all part of the hydrological cycle of the Amazon River basin. But since 2009, the waters in Anamã have been rising much higher than ever before. According to residents, the floods generally happen every other year, and there was a record-breaking deluge in 2015. Built on the banks of that same tiny tributary, Anamã's Hospital Francisco Salles de Moura has to be renovated annually: "Year in and year out, everything here goes underwater," says Dager Dourado, a general practitioner who lives midway between Anamã and Manaus. For doctors like him, the flooding affects his ability to attend to the local population as well as disrupts the hospital's operational routine.

In times of flood, the hospital is transferred to something like a floating medical barge. Despite this flexibility, the underlying structure of the main building is growing weaker year after year. Some equipment is fixed to the floor and cannot be transferred, leaving it submerged for months. The walls are showing profound cracks. "The hospital has been dealing with this since 2012," Dr. Dourado affirms. "A study of the river's fluctuations over time was done when it was built. They weren't having floods like these." When the waters recede, the costs of repair are immense.

The Tancredo Neves state school, which is also located on the banks of the river, has been completely rebuilt and "raised" to withstand the flooding. Luzinei Seixas de Oliveira, the security guard, said that "originally this school was at street level, so any sort of flooding we had would put it underwater. The biggest challenge was the building materials you lose."

The ways people have adapted their lives are most visible in the town's architecture. When the first floods occurred in 2005—and they weren't nearly as severe as those of 2009 and 2015—the locals began hastily to construct houses on stilts, creating intermediary floors or mezzanines in their homes and businesses. As the trend continued in the following years, many decided to build elevated homes, creating a peculiar architectural style in Anamã where very tall staircases are visible during the dry season. Others, perhaps the more ambitious, decided to turn their houses into floating houses.

Francisco Nunes Bastos, a member of the Party of National Mobilization (PMN), which opposes President Bolsonaro, is the town's mayor. Known by his nickname, Chico do Belo, he says at one time there was even a proposal to move the entire town from the floodplains further inland to solid ground in the Arixi region near Lake Anamã. But the people voted against it, because access to Arixi is practically impossible during the dry season. Afraid of putting so much work into a ghost town that would never be inhabited, the town abandoned its quixotic plan to abandon itself.

Escalating Floods and Droughts

Over the past decade, six cases of extreme flooding have been recorded in the Amazon region. Since measurements began being taken at the Port of Manaus in 1903, three of the five most severe floods occurred in the decade from 2009. In recent years, there has also been an increase in the amplitude between water levels during the two phases; in other words, the floods are increasingly severe, and the droughts are increasingly dry. Scientists are looking at rising temperatures in the surface waters of the Atlantic Ocean, resulting from unchecked global warming, as the possible cause of this potentially irreversible change to the Amazon ecosystem.

"With rising temperatures, more water evaporates from the ocean, resulting in more rain in the Amazon area," explains Marco Oliveira, a geologist and researcher with the

Geological Survey of Brazil (CPRM), under the jurisdiction of the Ministry of Mines and Energy. He goes on to explain that, because of the Earth's rotation, the trade winds blow from the Atlantic into the Amazon basin, bringing with them clouds of moisture evaporated from the ocean's surface. These clouds eventually reach the Andes mountains, essentially a six-thousand-meter-high barricade, and so the moisture rains down over the Amazon.

The rainforest doesn't create water, but rather "recycles" it, as Marco Oliveira puts it. This has a direct effect on the entire South American ecosystem. As the rainforest breathes and perspires, masses of humid air drift towards south-central parts of Brazil and its neighboring countries, bringing rain to these regions. This complex system, which depends on delicate relationships between the Earth's rotation, the ocean, geological formations, and vegetation, has been altered most likely by global warming and other impacts human beings have had on nature.

More intense and abundant rainfall in the Amazon is often accompanied by droughts in the southeast. There is still no consensus among researchers on an explanation for the phenomenon, but Oliveira hypothesizes that the deforestation of the Cerrado, a vast tropical savanna region southeast of the Amazon, is generating masses of hot, dry air that are preventing the transfer of moisture to the southeast.

Jochen Schöngart is a German forestry scientist and researcher with the Coordination of Research in Environmental Dynamics team, part of the National Institute for Research in Amazônia (INPA). He analyzes the growth rings of trees in order to trace the chronology and dynamics of water cycles in the Amazon, and he points to other factors that may be aggravating these cycles in the rainforest, which is marked by the increasing severity of both floods and droughts: the historical average has been just over ten meters, but on several occasions in recent decades, it has exceeded thirteen. This increase in flood heights is believed to be caused by the simultaneous warming of surface waters in the tropical Atlantic and the cooling of surface waters in the equatorial Pacific.

Low-frequency fluctuations, such as the Atlantic Multidecadal Oscillation and the Pacific Decadal Oscillation, which have hot and cold phases lasting from sixty-five to eighty years and forty to sixty years respectively, exert a powerful influence over the distribution of rainfall. The current warm Atlantic phase tends to result in severe droughts in the Amazon, as occurred in 2005 and 2010, whereas the colder Pacific phase lends itself to an increase in the frequency and magnitude of flooding.

Schöngart goes on to explain that changes in climate caused by the phenomena known as El Niño and La Niña also influence rain and water cycles in the Amazon. El Niño results from an unusual warming of cold Pacific waters, primarily off the coasts of Peru, Ecuador, and Chile. The warming creates unusual rains in the region, decreasing the precipitation index in the Amazon and thus increasing rains in southern and southeastern Brazil. La Niña is the reverse: the cold Pacific waters become even colder, resulting in more rain for the Amazon and less for the south and southeast.

For the scientist, this increase in both frequency and magnitude is cause for concern. The year 2012 broke records for flooding in Manaus: "We're talking about the largest river basin on the planet, representing almost 20 percent of the world's fresh water. So, yes, it's something to worry about," warns Schöngart, who also points to the effects of building hydroelectric plants on these water cycles.

As part of a group of researchers from universities in France, Chile, the United Kingdom, and Peru, Schöngart published a study in the September 2018, issue of the journal *Science Advances*, revealing an increase in the frequency of severe floods and droughts over the last two to three decades: the largest increase in the 113 years since records began.

The study showed that: "In the first part of the twentieth century, there were severe floods, with water levels exceeding twenty-nine meters (the reference point for declaring a state of emergency in Manaus) approximately every twenty years. Currently, extreme flooding is occurring, on average, every four years." That's a five-fold increase over the past century.

Decimated Fish Populations

During the dry season, which runs from July to November along the Solimões stretch of the Amazon River, the phenomena seen and felt by the Amazonian population may be more subtle. Because there is less water in total, there are higher concentrations of fecal bacteria in water used for daily activities. In other words, it may be more contaminated.

Another phenomenon, which I witnessed myself while reporting on this story, is the high rate of mortality for aquatic life in the waterway that connects the town of Anamã to the lake during droughts: hundreds of thousands of fish dying and leaving the water fetid. According to Jânio dos Santos Menezes, president of the local fishermen's association, "Every year black water flows from the lake, past the town, and into the Solimões River," killing thousands of fish by asphyxiation as the water "turns," becoming turbid and muddy. "This year," the fisherman continues, "since there was such heavy rain, the water also came in from the Solimões."

As the fish start to suffocate, it becomes easier to catch them. In two days, Jânio estimates that fifteen tons were caught. A single two-man canoe brought in eight hundred kilograms alone. "It happens every year, has been for a long time, but normally the fish are being pushed towards the Solimões. This time, they were trapped in the waterway," he concludes.

Experts aren't quite ready to claim a relationship between this phenomenon and a change in hydrological cycles, although this year the unseasonal rains did have unpredictable effects for the fishermen. Water levels in lakes tend to be higher than in the rivers, and as the water drains from the lakes, it brings part of the muddy lakebed with it.

"Silt can kill fish through asphyxiation by clogging their gills, or by a ripple effect in which plants and other primary producers die en masse from a lack of light, and as they decay, they leech oxygen from the water," explains Cássio Edelstein, an oceanographer and permaculturist. Another possibility has to do with the fact that lake water is "naturally anoxic"—in other words, it tends to have a lower oxygen concentration than the river—and "when the lake water mixes with the river, the oxygen levels are proportionally reduced," according to Edelstein.

For Giovani Cavalcanti Marinho, a researcher with the Mamirauá Institute for Sustainable Development and an expert in fishery management, this is "a natural phenomenon that happens every year in just about all lowland environments, and which is also known locally as the 'breaking down' of the water." According to Giovani, this happens when "decomposing organic material is washed down from the lake and starts consuming the oxygen in the water."

Don't Drink the Water

"Everyone who visits from somewhere else gets sick," says nurse Fabrícia Nunes Batalha. Whether it's the rainy season or the dry season, water quality in Anamã is terrible, and the subject of constant complaints by residents.

"In the morning, the water is just nasty, nasty, nasty. It reeks and it's full of rust," complains Nadione Correia Batalha. "The worst thing in this town is the water."

Here, those who can afford it buy mineral water for drinking, cooking, and even bathing. Those who don't have such financial resources will occasionally make use of the town's two main bathing options: the locker room in the Tancredo Neves school, and a spa near the Esmeralda Moura neighborhood, which is one of the areas most affected by the floods.

Luiz Ribeiro dos Santos, a local farmer, says the local well is where he gets the water he needs. "It's a blessing that sprinkles water across the entire town. If it wasn't for the well, it would be nearly impossible to get clean water. The pipes and plumbing here are all rusty."

Many residents will even add a few drops of chlorine to the well water, as even that may be contaminated by runoff from the outhouses. "Around here, not even the best available drinking water is any good," says Manoel Alves, another farmer. During a flood, the town hall will connect hoses to their faucets and run them outside the building so the local residents can have access to "good" water.

"This is a floodplain," Dr. Dourado points out. "The river and the surface soil are in a constant state of flux. The entire town could be destroyed by unstable ground."

For Marco Oliveira, the water conditions can be explained by the geology of this stretch of the river, which is relatively low compared to the heights reached in the Andes Mountains where it originates. "There is a significant amount of clay deposited in the river basin right here, and clay doesn't retain water," the geologist explains. According to him, there's no point digging superficial wells, as these only reach down to muddy waters. Much deeper wells, drilled a kilometer or more into the earth, are needed in order to access the clean waters of the Alter do Chão aquifer, which is found in the substrata across much of Amapá, Pará, and Amazonas.

As Luizinho Lelis de Chagas, a self-employed dockhand who works in Anamã hauling goods at the port, says, "The town is flooded, it's completely waterlogged, and yet it never stops."

A sergeant from with city's Military Police, who asked not to be identified, puts it another way: "Here, we're on dry land for six months, and underwater for the rest. The town just goes about its business despite the water." The sergeant went on to tell the story of a friend who died during the rainy season and had to be buried in Manacapuru, because the more they dug in Anamã's cemetery, the more water appeared. The town has been forced to relocate the cemetery twice already, and a third move will likely be necessary soon.

Oliveira points out that Anamã is the only municipality where, during times of flooding, the Civil Defense doesn't step in with sandbags and bridgework because the town itself has already adapted. The geologist praises Anamã's ability to evolve in the face of adversity, but adds that much remains to be done, specifically when it comes to basic sanitation and waste management, as well as making adjustments to public buildings such as the hospital.

There's nothing that suggests to researchers that this is a reversible or even temporary situation. Their working hypothesis is that the level of rainfall in the Amazon is intensifying. Climate change across the globe is affecting the populations of small towns in the heart of the Amazon rainforest on a daily basis, and the forecast, according to Marco Oliveira, is that we'll be seeing many more Anamãs in the years to come.

The Poison Fields

In the early 2000s, the land next to Seu Macaxeira's house was bought by a newly arrived man from southern Brazil. At first, Seu Macaxeira was happy with the arrival of this new neighbor, who seemed friendly enough and said he'd come to work the land. He introduced himself by saying what he really wanted was a quiet space to live in, and that in the south he'd had a lot of friction with his neighbors. The impression he gave was that he'd come to settle down. In mid-1999, Seu Macaxeira had moved to the community of Santos da Boa Fé, near the Curuá-Una highway, in Santarém, western Pará. He was happy with his farm there, which grew papaya, *cupuaçu*, soursop, potatoes, passion fruit, and so much manioc that he earned the nickname he still carries to this day (Seu Macaxeira translates as Mr. Manioc). With his produce, he raised four children. Not a drop of pesticide. At that time, on the eve of a new millennium, soy wasn't even on the horizon.

"At first he was a very good neighbor, but then he started buying up land," Mr. Manioc recalls. First the neighbor bought the plot behind his, followed by the one to his right. In 2002, he started clearing the surrounding brush. He promised those he had bought from that he'd be generating employment in the region. Little by little, Mr. Manioc found himself surrounded. The promised peace and tranquility did not result, nor did the jobs. Especially during the brush-clearing phase. During those days, the noise was the primary inconvenience. But then came the soy. "That's when the friction really started," he recalls.

Mr. Manioc could see the effects of his neighbor's pesticides on his children. "It burns the eyes, it burns the throat," he said. "It causes chronic fevers and headaches." Later, they began taking a toll on his own professional activities. "I was just a family farmer living on my papaya and manioc harvests. I felt like giving up. The poison was always there." His crops all but stopped bearing fruit; when they did, they weren't as wholesome as before. Leaves withered before the flowers bloomed. His family's health and livelihood were under attack.

One afternoon in 2007, early in the Amazonian summer, Mr. Manioc saw his neighbor spraying the poison. It was six o'clock in the afternoon, and the children were at home. Concerned, he went over to talk about the situation with him.

"I told him not to. I said if he didn't stop spraying that poison, I'd report him," recalls the farmer.

A few days later, also in the late afternoon, the neighbor came to visit him. He excused himself before saying, "Seu Antônio, I'm here today to offer you two business opportunities. Either you buy my land, or I buy yours."

Surrounded by property larger than his own, which had been environmentally degraded by the felling of the forest and the accumulation of pesticides, and with his economic stability undermined by his neighbor's activities, Mr. Manioc had no way of buying the land. "There was no way we could stay. Nobody could live there breathing in that soy with that poison. So I was forced to sell."

Mr. Manioc moved to Jacaré lane, another part of Santos da Boa Fé, which is where we conducted this interview. Since 2005, soy has taken over the community along with many others in the region known as Planalto Santareno, which includes the municipalities of Santarém, Belterra, and Mojuí dos Campos. "It's not the price of the land that forces people to hand over their lots. It's the poison," he says simply.

The Community of Boa Esperança

"Macaws and monkeys have been coming here for years to eat berries from the trees. They'd come right up to your front door. All of a sudden, they've disappeared," Sônia Maria Guimarães Sena, of the Boa Esperança community, says wistfully. She lives next to her father, Raimundo Alves Guimarães, also known as Seu Curica. The backyards of their two houses end where the soybean field begins. The two of them are surrounded, and the differences between the lands is remarkable: on one side of the fence, by the homes, you have a proliferation of species, including banana trees, cashew trees, lemon trees, manioc trees, and many others bearing various fruits. On the other side you have soy, corn, and glyphosate: the poison used to control the pests.

"Some people put up a fight, but they failed," Seu Curica recalls. "They [the soybean farmers] were buying up land here and there, and anyone caught in the middle of it was forced to sell because they couldn't afford it anymore. The poison kills everything, takes everything, covers everything. That's why they sold it all. They weren't able to plant their own crops anymore."

He shows me a cashew tree in his yard. "It's all just seeds. It blooms, but there's no fruit." As he has grown older, he has stopped working the fields, which were close to the Curuá-Una Hydroelectric Plant. Now retired, he spends his days weaving fishing nets. It's time-consuming work, and each net sells for six hundred *reais*.

His wife died from stomach cancer in May 2019, a few months before our visit. Maria Dercy Godinho is remembered by her family as a fighter. Both father and daughter get emotional when talking about her. "When she was alive, my wife fought hard to keep the pesticides out of here. But it didn't work." We walked through the cemetery where she's buried, just a few meters from the house in which she lived. The cemetery itself is surrounded by a flat, monochromatic expanse of grain fields.

"The smell that came in was so strong it made her nauseous. She had trouble breathing; she was always short of breath. She shut herself inside the house, waiting for the pesticide to go, to blow away. That was her problem, the shortness of breath. She protested, she got the people together to see if they would hold out and refuse to sell their land. She got the union people involved. But in the end, they sold. There was just no other way. Money spoke the loudest," Seu Curica reflects, looking lost in some distant, uncertain place.

Maria Dercy Godinho had been a member of the Santarém Rural Workers Union, as was Seu Macaxeira. This union is at the forefront of the fight against soy and the impact it's having in the region.

One of Seu Curica's neighbors declined to be interviewed. "I don't want any problems," he said. "Why would I bad-mouth the soybean company when they're renting my land? I even get a little bit of glyphosate," he added. This tall, clear-eyed soy farmer from Rio Grande do Sul started crunching the numbers and talking about how hard it would have been for him to continue his business making and selling manioc flour. He wanted to demonstrate, mathematically, that the most logical and profitable option for small, rural landowners was to rent their property to the big soybean farming corporations. According to him, a sack of manioc flour can be sold for eighty *reais* at the market in downtown Santarém. But when you compare that with a twenty *reais* shipping fee to cover the forty-kilometer distance separating Boa Esperança from the city, "It's just not worth it," as he says. Instead, by renting out the land for cultivating soy, you get a fixed income regardless of productivity. "If I had a hundred hectares," he figured out loud, adding everything up, "I could rent out seventy and live on the income."

Later, Mr. Manioc and I made our way to the Ramal da Moça community. "Ever since 2005, the locals have really been hit hard," he said as we approached the place. He wanted to show me what was left of the community, especially the abandoned homes of residents who had sold everything and moved to the city. To his surprise, most of these had already been torn down. Seventy-five families had once lived on this land. Now there was nothing but soy. All that remained were two houses and the school, which were already covered by undergrowth climbing the walls and wrapping the buildings in a green mantle. Soon, they too would be taken down.

Soy creates a change in the relationship between people and the land on which they live. It enforces an effect of separation and removal; the locals are forced to abandon their communities and head for the city. Single-crop grain farming doesn't leave anything untouched: it has unequivocally changed the landscape, life, and social relationships in Planalto Santareno.

"There's no hope of doing better for yourself here, because everything's shut down," Seu Curica laments. "There's no way to move up, to move forward." What corporate soybean operations call development means ruin for small, local farmers. There's a general feeling of discouragement and resignation in the air, which contrasts sharply with the community's name: Boa Esperança, or Good Hope. It's a place to which many people flocked when the forest began to open up in the early 1930s. There was a promising future there based on the extraction of rosewood for the production of perfume. Just a few years later, the name seemed to fit rather well with the quality of life. The community had become an important producer of flour for Santarém. "There were so many jobs here. You didn't go around looking for positions, they came looking for you," Seu Curica says, referring to a distant past that's nowhere to be found in the community today. "When the soybeans showed up, people started selling their land, and the jobs dried up."

The Maicá Lake

Ciro de Souza Brito is a lawyer working for Terra de Direitos, an NGO that provides legal advice to rural and *quilombola* communities affected by the encroachment of soy in the Planalto Santareno region. "Soy doesn't just show up by itself, as a commodity," he says. "It brings plenty of problems along with it. It tends to deterritorialize, it criminalizes, it marginalizes, and it will make you sick."

The lawyer quickly articulates his points, making their connections clear and explaining the seriousness of the situation. He analyzes the expansion of the soy network in the region starting with its impact on those living closest to the land itself:

"As soy production expands, it deterritorializes communities and increases the need to dispatch all the produce that's being harvested. Where will it go? This raises the question of the Maicá lake. The local communities know it's a breeding ground for fish. Even Dileudo says so. And studies have shown it's a fish sanctuary that includes over eighteen species. It's a place where birds come to feed on fish. The lake and the surrounding areas are very rich in biodiversity."

Dileudo Guimarães dos Santos, president of the Quilombo do Bom Jardim residents' association, understands the reality of the Maicá lake better than most. He has felt the impact not only of the soy plantation itself but also of the infrastructure required to ship out the beans. We met him at the *quilombo* where Black Awareness Day was already in full swing, and came back to interview him forty-eight hours later. The *quilombo* was still in a party mood, although the festivities were winding down and people were tidying the common areas and returning to their daily activities.

Quilombo do Bom Jardim is located in a place that's difficult to access, tucked between the Maicá lake and the base of a mountain range. To get there, if you're coming from the Curuá-Una highway, you need to take the side roads flanked by hectares of soybean fields, pass by Mr. Manioc's land, and descend a steep and slippery ravine. For Dileudo, the *quilombo*'s location is strategic:

"The people who came here, who first came here as slaves, situated themselves down there, but some of them spent the day working up in the mountains, where it offered a better view of the river. That way, they could warn people by calling out, 'Hey, there's a boat, someone's coming.'"

In the interior of Pará, history is repeating itself in a curious way. It seems to have reversed the famous phrase often used by historians. In Tapajós land, history happens first as a farce, and then as a tragedy. In this specific location, once favorable to those fleeing slavery, the *quilombo* now receives water laced with poison from the soy plantations that sit atop the mountain. Contaminants are also being leached into the water supply from a landfill high above the city of Santarém. Despite taking action to get a title to their land, squatters are encroaching on their territory and planting soybeans. Meanwhile, few of the *quilombolas* themselves "have any land to work," Dileudo says, regretfully.

In addition to the poor water quality, he is also concerned about the fish. "This is Tapajós water. In the Amazon, it's more whitish," Dileudo says. "We've noticed this water is starting to change color, and dead fish are starting to turn up. We think it's due to contamination, and we know that contaminated water reduces the fish population."

He fears that the construction of ports and increased traffic from barges and other larger vessels could churn up sand and mud from the bottom of the Maicá River. And this implies an even greater problem for the security of the *quilombolas'* food supply: with the deforestation that growing soy requires, hunting has taken a hit. As Dileudo explains, "Hunting really depends on the forest. Animals depend on fruit. If the forest goes away, obviously the birds, monkeys, paca, agoutis, all sorts of game, and even the trees themselves, will try to find somewhere else to live." Brazil-nut and bacabeira trees are among those being felled, further weakening the *quilombolas'* food supply.

Meanwhile, the soy fields continue to grow unabated. Brito has been closely following the construction of the Ferro Grão railroad, as well as the Teles Pires–Tapajós waterway project. The lawyer points to the relationship between the development of infrastructure to transport soybean harvests across midwestern Brazil and the incentive for production in the Planalto Santareno region:

"The Cargill port, which primarily facilitates the shipping of much of the production coming from Mato Grosso and the surrounding areas, all part of this 'Arco Norte' that connects middle and western Brazil with the north, granting access to the ocean, really encouraged planting around here. And there's a plan for six port terminals to be constructed on the Maicá lake for private use. Besides shipping out what's already being grown, it will also serve as an incentive for local and foreign growers to come invest here."

Brito sees a number of favorable conditions for the construction of private ports on the Maicá lake: water depth, easy road access, as well as a direct connection to the Amazon River in an area where the currents are stronger. All of these factors, both natural and political, are the basis of persuasive lobbying to change the city of Santarém's master plan.

"Lake Maicá and the surrounding region is an environmental preservation area. You couldn't do anything there. So when it came to changing the municipal master plan, there was a whole year of public debate, consultations and hearings. Communities and social movements and other organizations emphasized the need to keep this area protected. That seemed to be how it was all working out. So we thought, in the end, when the new master plan was approved and made into law, it would all remain a protected area," Brito says.

"Then a group of lobbyists got involved," he continues. "In December, when everyone was happy, the Chamber and the City Hall approved a plan that actually designated this area for port expansion." A separate part of the plan addressed soy specifically: virtually all land that wasn't already designated as an environmental preservation area would be open to the development of monocropping.

As the protocol for their consultation hadn't been respected, the *quilombolas* went to court, which temporarily halted construction of the ports. However, a separate project—a ship refueling terminal with all the proper municipal and state authorizations in order—is being built, and with it, the entire logistical infrastructure. "They're moving forward with the port," Ciro says. "Everything's coming together. Construction is being completed."

A Farce

We travel by car between the rural communities along the Curuá-Uná highway. Mr. Manioc is with us, explaining what the region was like before the arrival of soy compared with today.

"These communities are a farce!" he exclaims, from the back seat.

"What do you mean?" I ask.

"There's just a few houses here and there along the road. That's it. Nothing else. Before, it was an actual community."

A few kilometers further down the road, he resumes his reasoning: "The farce is what they left behind," he says, pointing to the last few narrow strips of rainforest remaining in a vast expanse of soybean fields. "Just a few trees here and there. Everything else is soy," he concludes.

He explains that all these people sold their land for pennies on the dollar. Humble farmers who lived off what they grew were deluded by offers of just ten or fifteen thousand *reais*. They thought it would be enough to start a new life in the city; instead, they now find themselves living in poverty. The money ran out in a year or two at most. Unlike life in the rural communities, everything in the city comes at a price. Mr. Manioc sums it up: "First we went through the era of coffee barons. Today, they're soy barons."

Manoel Edivaldo Santos Matos is known as "O Peixe"— "The Fish." He's a traditional farmer and president of the Santarém Rural Workers' Union. He recalls the arrival of soy in the region: in the late 1990s and early 2000s, the city mayor invited soy producers from other parts of Brazil, especially Mato Grosso state, to conduct a test on a single hectare of land. Rice, beans, fruit, and manioc were already being grown. "And soy worked well. It really started to flourish here.

"Growers from Mato Grosso poured into the region. They even created a real estate consortium. When the company men showed up, they'd go around buying up all the land," O Peixe says.

He joined the union's board of directors in July 2002, when the rush to sell land to soy producers began. In October that year, they took a quick survey to understand the impact of this new situation: "Six hundred farmers had already sold their land," O Peixe says. That was when they started their first "Don't give up your land" campaign. "That gave us a bit of breathing room, but not enough," O Peixe laments. "The lobby behind the buyouts was just too big."

Then came the Cargill port. The president of the union at the time was Dona Ivete Bastos, who flew to Europe to highlight what was going on in the region, to show European soy buyers the impact of monocropping in the region: "Back then, there wasn't much talk about the impact of poisons. It was more about the expulsion of farmers. It was about streams getting blocked up with fallen trees," says O Peixe. According to him, Cargill had failed to carry out an environmental impact study before beginning construction on the port, and were forced to adapt on the fly.

These were the circumstances around which negotiations for a moratorium on soy products began. For O Peixe, it was largely due to pressure from the American fast food company

McDonald's, which didn't want to feed their chickens with soybeans harvested from deforested land. The moratorium was agreed by producers, consumers, and environmental organizations alike.

"The agreement was that Europe would only buy soy grown in legally designated areas," O Peixe recalls. "Areas local farmers hadn't been kicked out of, that didn't have an environmental impact on streams and whatnot, and where old-growth trees hadn't been cut down to create fields. Just altered or degraded areas, as they say."

But later they failed to comply, and the situation worsened.

O Peixe remains skeptical about promises made by the agribusiness sector, which claims that ports, railroads, and highways will be a boon to the municipality.

"That story just doesn't hold water anymore. We know that where this is going on, there are those who do very well by it. But for the majority of the population it has a negative effect: it increases poverty, it increases misery, it increases hunger, public insecurity, and violence. It concentrates income, it concentrates land, and generally has a negative impact on society . . . especially when it comes to health."

O Peixe quotes from a speech given by Erik Jennings, a doctor in Santarém, about the local population's future health: it's a sickly one, due to ingesting fish contaminated with mercury and to exposure to pesticides. In April 2019, Dr. Jennings attended a public hearing in the Chamber of Deputies, Brazil's federal legislative body, in Brasília. There, he gave a presentation to politicians and Indigenous people about the danger mercury presents to the Tapajós region. "My thesis is that the Amazonian people are sicker and more at risk than the rainforest," he said.

Development

Sérgio Schwade is Director of Agriculture with the Rural Union of Santarém, an entity representing the agricultural industry in the Planalto Santareno region. A landowner and agricultural engineer, his views differ from those of the small-scale farmers who are feeling the effects of the soy.

We talked at the union hall, where he expressed his opinion regarding the importance of agribusiness for development in the region. According to Schwade, the area used for grain production in Planalto Santareno is 75,000 hectares shared by 230 individual growers, yielding, on average, individual lots of 326 hectares each. "In the agricultural sector, that's considered a small property. It's practically family farming." He envisions the possibility of expanding productive lands in the area and intensifying them; that is, using technology to increase the productivity of existing local farmlands instead of deforesting new areas. "We have anthropized areas. We follow the moratorium on soy. So when there's some kind of improvement, some cleanup, for instance, the whole area needs to be divided up into parcels. Which means doing the business part in a legal way. There's lots of land, and we can expand without any problem."

Schwade and I discuss some complaints from traditional, rural farmers about the lack of jobs, that the promise of employment in the soy industry doesn't seem to be paying off. His answer suggests a different path:

"There's enough land for everyone around here. There's over seven hundred thousand hectares of human-use forest. Today, grain farmers are using only 10 percent of that. So there's plenty of land for everyone to work. If someone sells a plot here, he can go to town and start his business there. If he sells his entire farm, he can go to another location with more fertile land. Maybe his soil was exhausted, which is a natural process. Either way, you can have your land. A family farmer who wants to stay in business will stay in business. If he doesn't want to stay in the farming business, whether it's because he's getting up in age or doesn't have anyone to pass the farm on to, then, yes, they'll head to the city to study or something. But if someone's interested in farming, there's definitely space to do it. Now if the number of family farms drops from thirteen or whatever to six or three, that's not unreasonable," Schwade argues.

He also believes that new infrastructure will generate greater productivity and expand business opportunities in the region. "When I talk about infrastructure, I'm not just talking about the grain sector," he says. "I'm talking about the entire chain, the whole agriculture industry. Grains, meat, fish-farming. Because once you have a port in place, you can verticalize what you're producing here. It verticalizes the entire food production sector: you can start with vegetable protein, move to animal protein, and increase your income even more."

A few weeks before our conversation, NASA released a study with international implications on drought in the Amazon caused by human activity. "Over the last twenty years, the atmosphere above the Amazon rainforest has been drying out, increasing the demand for water and leaving ecosystems vulnerable to fires and drought. It also shows that this increase in dryness is primarily the result of human activities," it begins. "Scientists observed that the most significant and systematic drying of the atmosphere is in the southeast region, where the bulk of deforestation and agricultural expansion is happening." This is precisely where Planalto Santareno is located.

Citing this study, we asked Schwade if the soy industry was even slightly concerned about drought affecting their productivity in the Amazon. "We don't agree with those findings," he says. "At the National Institute for Space Research's meteorological station in Belterra, we averaged 1,903 millimeters of precipitation between 1967 and 1997. Today, we're over 2,000 millimeters. We've hit that mark several times. Even during the dry period." For Schwade, "That microclimate, that situation, that's just not how it is here."

When it comes to the poison, his belief is that, if proper negotiations are held between the two parties, a peaceful coexistence can be achieved.

"The rural growers here buy the product with a prescription that states you need to use X milliliters per hectare. It's especially important because, if you use more than that, you'll see losses. Plus, it's harmful. Just like medicine: if you double or triple the dosage, it becomes toxic. So we're very careful about not overdoing it. Now, when the treatment is done manually, it can be hard to measure, and often the amount ends up too concentrated. Today, there's equipment that does all the measurements, resulting in the most accurate, most correct dose. There's a lot of training and guidance that comes with it."

Which led us to Seu Curica and his poisoned cashew tree. We asked if there was any sort of monitoring or oversight by the union. Schwade's response was that it's not the union's job to conduct inspections.

"We're not inspectors, we don't go around checking on things, and there's no way to know what all the growers might be applying at any given moment. So we just don't know what's happening. You need to listen to both sides, and neighbors need to have that understanding as well: when one person is growing something, the other doesn't apply a particular product, and vice versa. You have to have this dialogue: when my tree is blooming, don't use certain products. I believe we can come to this understanding, and everyone can be a part of it."

Poison and Schools

I arrived at Belterra's Vitalina Motta school early in the afternoon. The children were still in class, and a red tractor was working freely in the soybean field opposite the school facilities. The teachers and administrators, almost all women, wanted to talk about the situation, but were also apprehensive. Several asked that we only record their voices, anonymously, considering the tension in the daily relationship between teachers, students, and poison: terms that should never be used in the same sentence.

Heloíse Rocha, an Indigenous teacher, was willing to give a full interview. She's been working in the Trevo de Belterra school district for five years; for three, she was teaching at a neighboring school, which was also surrounded by soybean fields, and for the last two years she's been with Vitalina Motta. She says there was never any negotiation with the farmers about not spraying the fields during school hours. "There was no discussion. The school board never debated this. I made an official request. I said, 'We have to do something. We need to protect our children and protect ourselves.'"

She reports that the spraying is being done at any time of day and without any sort of announcement or warning. One of the challenges is containing the students' innate inquisitiveness. With the tractors running so close to school property, many of the children want to see them in action while teachers try to keep their charges at bay. "They're curious, and that gives them a face-first exposure to the application," Heloíse adds. There are also concerns about contaminants possibly making their way into the school's water supply, which comes from a hand-built well and runs through a filtration system. "We know that the pesticides leach into the water table," she says. But no tests on water quality have been done. The limited number of studies is, in fact, one of the biggest problems for the people of Planalto Santareno's understanding of the poison. The impact is simply unknown.

As Rocha puts it, "At the school, we feel like hostages." She and the rest of the staff seem to harbor no doubts about the dangers they're facing. "Everyone who works here agrees that we're being contaminated. We may not be feeling the full effects yet. Just a few people who are more sensitive, who have less immunity. But regardless, little by little, we're being poisoned."

We reached out to the Belterra Department of Education in hopes they would comment on the students' exposure to pesticides, but they didn't respond to our queries.

Kalysta de Oliveira Resende is an oncologist and hematologist with privileges at both the Hospital Regional do Baixo Amazonas and the Oncológica do Brasil clinic, both in Santarém, where we were able to talk. She works with secondary prevention as well as early detection and treatment of cancer. For these reasons, she is often called upon by the Santarém Rural Workers Union to give public talks on the dangers of handling pesticides and on care for those who've been exposed.

This is not to say that one thing implies the other. As the doctor goes on to explain, "Nobody is saying that all patients who are exposed to pesticides will end up developing cancer. Especially because the process of carcinogenesis is such a long one and involves genetic mutations. But we do know that exposure to pesticides can be a predisposing factor." She also notes that, in addition to cancer, there are other health risks at play. In the short term, there can be acute pathologies, usually allergic reactions such as coughing, sneezing, and redness in the eyes, but there is also the possibility of more serious neurological and pulmonary implications. With long-term exposure, besides cancer, there are increased risks of endocrine disorders and of infertility.

Dr. Resende explains that 80 percent of cancer cases involve environmental factors of some sort. Exposure to pesticides is one that can be mitigated. Therefore, her primary focus is on prevention and education. She lists measures which she believes will help prevent the development of cancer caused by pesticide exposure. "By encouraging organic agriculture, family farming, and the search for technologies and techniques other than pesticides, we can really alter the course of history," she says.

In order for Dr. Resende's rather optimistic bet to pay off, many changes need to be made.

Effects on the Forest

Heloíse Rocha is adamant that soy has taken over Belterra. Not only in the rural areas, but in urban spaces as well. And the drone images we captured show how right she is: the soybean fields spread right up against the edge of the Tapajós National Forest which, by law, can no longer be felled or clear-cut.

As a resident of Piquiatuba, Remerson Castro Almeida lives in one of fifteen riverside communities within the protected area, along with three Indigenous Munduruku villages: Bragança, Marituba, and Takuara. They're separated from the soy fields by roughly fifty kilometers of dense rainforest where the local population goes to hunt, often coming across jaguar tracks. Still, though, the impacts of soy production are being felt. "Bugs we never knew existed" have started to appear in the community, most likely fleeing the poison. In 2019, preparations for the açaí festival had to be halted because the lighting equipment attracted insects never seen before in this community.

"If that forest were still standing, all these insects wouldn't be coming here," Remerson reflects. Another change is the increasing heat, which makes it more difficult to stay out working in the fields. "In the past, if we headed out at six in the morning, we could hold out until eleven-thirty or twelve," Remerson says. "Nowadays, we make it till ten at the latest. As family farmers, losing even that hour or two per day is cutting into our production."

At the time of the Tapajós National Forest's formal designation, in 1974, as an Environmental Conservation Unit, there was a major mobilization of the residents, for the military government wanted a forest without people. But the locals refused to leave, sparking a struggle for the right to stay, which many of the older residents still remember.

Despite this, Remerson describes a degree of uncertainty over the continuation of communities in the National Forest. A land-use concession contract established in 2010 is, as the name suggests, a concession, a "loan," as Remerson puts it. "What will happen to us when this concession ends? What will happen to us if the government wants to go back and change the law?" he worries.

This concern only increased when President Bolsonaro's administration presented a list of sixty-seven conservation units to be reduced or eliminated. Among them is the Tapajós National Forest. The justification, according to the government, is to ensure legal security for government projects, especially infrastructure, such as federal roads, railways, shipping ports, and airports. When asked to comment, ICMBio did not respond.

"For we who live here today, who live off of sustainability . . . we depend on the land, we collect what we need," Remerson summarizes. "That's how we survive. And now our future is in doubt. Will the laws that protect us remain in place, or will they be replaced by laws that favor big business? It's basically a struggle between the poor and very wealthiest." The overarching fear is that everything will be transformed into soy, and that the destiny of Boa Esperança will be repeated in Piquiatuba and the other rainforest communities.

Where to Go

Mr. Manioc left his land in Santos da Boa Fé after he found himself hemmed in by his neighbor's land in the early 2000s. He says that when he moved to Jacaré lane, the place was all jungle. "There was nothing around here," he recalls. Yet he and his children, who are now grown, find themselves surrounded again. His property resembles many others we saw in the region: where your yard ends, the monocropping begins. No wall, no separation whatsoever. Ironically, his only protection now is his own manioc trees which border the expansive fields of soy.

"It's suffocating," Mr. Manioc says. And yet he excitedly envisions an alternative. "The only way to counter single-crop farming is for us to work organically," he says. "To have a large-scale organic operation." He expects, though, that the Bolsonaro administration will do everything possible to derail family farming and organic agriculture.

He can no longer guarantee that his own produce is free from poisons. "The wind is at their backs," as he puts it. Other farmers admit that, with the pesticides being spread across the soy fields, they have been forced to use the same chemicals on their own farms. Otherwise, they'll never stand a chance. Poison begets more poison.

Having lived in the region for twenty-eight years, Seu Macaxeira does not mince his words. "Their goal is to end our community," he says bluntly. His story is the story of all people subjected to the cold laws of market competition. There are frequent accusations of land grabbing and squatting, which have been decried by people like Dileudo, from the Bom Jardim *quilombo*. But in many other cases, land purchases are carried out in accordance with all the current legislation. The same goes for poison use. Not breaking the law, however, does not mean this isn't a violent process. With every square meter of land acquired, with each forested plot that's felled in favor of single-crop grains, with every gallon of poison that's sprayed, the small rural farmers are increasingly driven to the brink. Eventually they become exiles. They flee to the city. Or they simply remain, like Seu Curica's cashew trees: listless, unable to bear fruit, out of touch with the land to which they once belonged.

"So where do I go now? Where am I going to find land? I thought maybe along the BR-163 highway, but there's nothing there. I thought about Curuá-Una, but there's nothing there either. I thought about Lago Grande, but the agribusinesses are already there, and nothing's left. . . ." The first time he found himself cornered by the soy, Mr. Manioc had somewhere to go. He got himself a plot of land adjacent to the same community and filled with forest. Now, he sees no way out. In fact, here, deep in the state of Pará, history seems to be repeating itself: first as farce, and then as a tragedy.

"Nature Herself Is Drying Up": A *Quilombo* on the Marajó Archipelago Feels the Impact of Rice Paddies amid Turbulent Times

Life and water are practically synonymous. If it's true that water governs life in every part of the world, then in the case of the Marajó Archipelago in Pará, the aphorism acquires an even greater degree of truth. In this group of islands set between the mouth of the Amazon River and the Atlantic Ocean, periods of rain and drought define life to such an extent that Rosivaldo Moraes Correa, a mathematics teacher at the Comunidade de Remanescentes do Quilombo Gurupá school, in Cachoeira do Arari, one of Marajó's sixteen municipalities, talks about a "dictatorship of water." The expression is a reference to *Marajó: a ditadura da água*, a book by Italian priest Giovanni Gallo, who spent part of his life there on the archipelago:

> On Marajó it is not the national president, nor the governor, who reigns. Here, there is an absolute and total dictatorship: water. It is water that offers the means of subsistence and impedes life; it conditions health, work, everything, without raising its voice in a disloyal, ruthless manner. The seasons of the year have different names: water, mud, drought. It is a dictatorship of water.

Today, however, the waters flowing around Cachoeira do Arari are being impacted by external agents with the power of an earthquake: water poisoned by the intensive pesticide use, escaped animals, and the previously inconceivable drying up of streams coupled with Marajó's drastic transformation into a focus for rice cultivation.

Correa explains how the water cycle is governed by two primary forces: the tides, which dictate the daily opportunities for moving from house to house, which can only be done by boat, and the seasons, characterized by high levels of rainfall in the winter and droughts in the summer.

As the crow flies, only seventy-one kilometers separate Cachoeira do Arari from Belém, the capital of Pará. But the trip is a long one and involves a torturous ferry crossing, which itself can last three hours, between Belém and Salvaterra, a municipality next to Cachoeira do Arari. Until a few years ago, the *quilombo* could only be reached by boat. Today you can get there via a branch of the road that connects Cachoeira do Arari with Salvaterra. This winds through side roads, crossing rice paddies and open fields where buffalo range freely, often right into the road, all of which demands great caution from the driver.

Little by little, the vegetation begins to change. The savanna grows thicker until it reaches the *quilombolas'* territory, which is surrounded by dense forest and açaí groves. On part of that territory, along the Gurupá River, there's an area of solid ground where some of the 850 or so families that make up the *quilombo* live. It occupies an area of eleven thousand hectares, divided into seven sectors, which together form a single community. In addition to this bit of terra firma, there's also a fertile floodplain region perfect for açaí palms, which stretches along the Arari River and its beautiful streams—winding water courses edged by leaning trees.

Rice paddies have impacted life in Quilombo Gurupá since 2010, when agriculturalist and politician Paulo César Quartiero arrived here to expand his rice business. According to the *quilombolas*, the impacts have been many and multifaceted. Originally from Rio Grande do Sul, Quartiero built a port in territory claimed by the *quilombolas*, without their consent. The rice paddies attract ducks and geese, drawing them away from *quilombo* territory. The birds' departure has influenced both the ecosystem and the locals' food supply: in addition to losing an important source of protein—duck is traditional in Paraense cuisine—they also lost the birds' predators. In order to protect his rice, Quartiero uses pesticides that can reach the *quilombo* though the rivers and streams. And finally, in order to irrigate the paddies, water is siphoned off from the mouth of the Arari River, drying up streams and affecting spawning of the fish. The açaí groves, a primary source of income for the *quilombolas*, have also begun to dry up, though the locals don't know why.

"We're here at the mouth of the Arari River. When it comes to the rice-growing in and around Cachoeira do Arari, and the arrival of Quartiero, who has a business venture that's tied to the municipal center, just off highway PA-154, you might be thinking, 'It's far enough away from the *quilombolas*' territory; it shouldn't have any effect.' But we believe it does have an effect. A direct one," Correa declares.

I visited the Quilombo Gurupá community in early January 2020. Correa was adamant in condeming the effects of pesticides in the area. This is a reality that plagues not only the *quilombo* but many small, traditional communities in the Amazon. "It's applied by air. Every day, for as long as they're germinating. That's the period they consider necessary," he says. "Everyone is a witness because everyone sees it as they're driving down PA-154. Sometimes, if you're riding a motorcycle, you get soaked in it."

He also says there's intensive use of chemicals to dry out Quartiero's rice fields. Sometimes, when Correa goes to the city on an errand, the vegetation is green. When he returns to the *quilombo* a few hours later, it's completely dried out and ready for harvesting. "There's just no other word for all of this," he says: "It's poison."

The teacher fears that all the pesticide-laced water will filter directly into the *quilombo*. "Here in the Amazon, in the middle of the winter, the water only comes down, so whatever's up there comes down with it," he says. "Of course, it goes straight to Arari, and has a direct impact on us here," he adds, fearing that the fish and shrimp, two important foods for the *quilombolas*, may well be contaminated.

According to Correa, no in-depth studies have been conducted to determine the impact of pesticides in the region. What he does know is that nobody was informed of the imminent arrival of large-scale rice production. A study done by the Evandro Chagas Institute back in 2013 didn't find excessive levels of pesticides in the water used to irrigate Quartiero's farm. But no samples were taken in the *quilombo*, which is where much of the runoff from the rice paddies accumulates.

Rosivaldo Correa then points to yet another threat posed by rice production. During the summer months with lower rainfall, rice farmers draw the water they need from the Arari River. "They take millions of liters of water from the river to irrigate the rice." Which is why Correa believes that the Arari and its tributaries are starting to run dry.

"The channels we once used aren't there anymore. Since I had a boat for transporting things, I just got tired of trying to get through that part of the territory. We used to always go to Cachoeira [do Arari]. But now, the channel I used to know just doesn't exist," he says.

Alfredo Neto Batista da Cunha, who left his role as president of the Remanescentes do Quilombo Gurupá community association in 2020, is emphatic about the drought. "The impact runs deep through the river. Nature herself is drying up once and for all." He goes on to link the drought to the decrease in fish and shrimp: "The populations are dropping. That's what we're seeing the most. The Laranjeira used to be such a deep river . . . but today, if you're not careful, you can get stranded right in the middle of it."

Quartiero was one of the rice farmers forced out of the Raposa Serra do Sol Indigenous Territory in Roraima. On March 19, 2009, Brazil's Supreme Federal Court confirmed the demarcation of 1.7 million hectares could only be inhabited by Indigenous people, upholding the original decree made by President Luiz Inácio Lula da Silva in 2005. This was intended to end conflicts with the Ingarikó, Makuxi, Patamona, Taurepang, and Wapishana people, among others: a problem that had plagued the region since the 1970s.

Quartiero was born in Torres, Rio Grande do Sul, in 1952. He first came to Roraima in the early 2000s and quickly bought a number of farms. From 2005 to 2008 he served as mayor of Pacaraima for a center-right political party. During his term, he was accused of a number of crimes against Indigenous people, including one incident in which he ordered his ranch employees to open fire on a group of Makuxi in 2008.

The Indigenous people were holding a protest, calling for rice farmers' immediate departure from the land, when shots were fired. Ten people were injured, three of them seriously. Quartiero was arrested shortly thereafter and spent nine days in the Federal Police jail in Brasília on charges of conspiracy and illegal possession of explosive devices. Upon his release, he returned to Roraima, to a welcome party thrown by admirers and sympathetic politicians.

Continuing his career as a politician, the rice farmer served as a federal representative from 2011 and 2015, and later as vice-governor of the state from 2015 and 2018.

Quartiero started his business in Marajó a year after pulling out of the Raposa Serra do Sol Indigenous territory. In 2010, he bought the Reunida Espírito Santo and Santa Lourdes farms, situated between the municipalities of Cachoeira do Arari and Salvaterra, for roughly $380,000. Together, the two properties total 12,580 hectares.

He also held a 90 percent share in the Quartiero Almeida company (also known as Acostumado Alimentos Ltda or Arroz Acostumado), which had a market cap of $175,000 until 2014. But, according to records *Amazônia Real* obtained from the Board of Trade, he handed over control of the company to his family members Ericina de Almeida Quartiero, who manages the family business in Boa Vista, and Larissa de Almeida Quartiero, a lawyer in Florianópolis. The Reunida Espírito Santo and Santa Lourdes farms are registered in the name of his son, Renato de Almeida Quartiero.

Elielson Pereira da Silva worked at INCRA for nearly a decade, and has come to know thirteen of the sixteen municipalities that make up the archipelago. He understands the reality of the situation in Marajó well, despite not being born there. As INCRA's Regional Superintendent, his arrival coincided with that of the rice farmers.

"Everything suggests that the appropriation of this land happened in a completely illegal, illegitimate way," Da Silva says. "If you've got the money, you could buy the entire state of Pará. Yes, it's true. There's no legal or constitutional provision preventing this, as long as you get legislative authorization from the National Congress for anything over twenty-five hundred hectares. Back then, in 2010, Quartiero listed his land at twelve thousand hectares. Where is the authorization allowing for Quartiero, or whoever it may be, to buy up that much land in Marajó?"

The argument Da Silva made in 2010 was finally confirmed in August 2019, when the Public Prosecutor's Office for the State of Pará successfully revoked the registration of Quartiero's lands. In a public statement, the prosecutor's office announced that, "In considering this case, and all the documents presented by the defense, Judge André Filo-Creão da Fonseca rules that the proceedings do not indicate the specific moment at which the transfer of these properties from public ownership to the private domain would have taken place, thus depriving the previous owners of their right to proceed, through normal means, with the sale of the properties."

Da Silva sums up the legalese in this way: "When Quartiero arrived, he had no legal authority [to do what he did]. Public lands were not being allocated. He had no legal ground to stand on." He also points out that certain damages could have been avoided, arguing that "it took eight years to get the result we'd been arguing for from the very beginning."

The new president of the Remanescentes do Quilombo Gurupá community association, Maria de Fátima Gusmão

Batista, confirms that they were never consulted or otherwise contacted regarding the arrival of the rice farmers.

"At no time were we ever consulted about Quartiero's arrival. He just showed up, started buying up the land, getting his hands on it, and he's been working it ever since. It wasn't very neighborly to just swoop in and set up next to us like that."

What Does Quartiero Say?

In an interview with *Amazônia Real*, Paulo César Quartiero denied having legal problems with the Comunidade de Remanescentes do Quilombo Gurupá. "I don't know. That community is far away. Almost seventy kilometers," he says, claiming that there's no interference or territorial conflict. "The farm belongs to a family that's been in the region for a century or more, so there's no problem there."

When asked about his use of Caracará port, Quartiero defends himself, saying it's open to the public. "It's a public port. Anyone can use it. It's for the community," he says.

"Here's the situation," Quartiero goes on. "We're planting. We have the largest plantation. It's ours. So we're planting here. In Brazil, the problem is that big growers like us are always seen as suspicious, as criminals, when in fact we're employers. We've had the privilege of being harassed. Not just in Marajó, but in Roraima and the rest of the country. But fortunately, Brazil is starting to change. It used to be the people doing nothing were the heroes, while the growers were the bad guys. Now, that's changing a bit."

This "change" in Brazilian politics was the election of extreme right-wing presidential candidate Jair Bolsonaro in 2018. Quartiero's insinuation—that the Labor Party, which governed Brazil during the administrations of Lula da Silva and Dilma Rousseff, harassed and oppressed large-scale farms across the country—is clear.

Amazônia Real asked Quartiero whether he saw the change as positive or negative. "Do you think it's better to be like Venezuela?" he replied. "Of course not. Better production means better development. Marajó has the worst Human Development Index (HDI) in Brazil. Of the ten municipalities with the worst HDI, three are in Marajó, including the worst one, Melgaço. But here we are, contributing to development, paying taxes, and creating jobs."

As a final note, the rice farmer adds that he has, in total, "over a hundred" employees working his land. He agreed to this interview on February 27, 2020.

Where the Conflict Began

Since the 1970s, residents of the Quilombo Gurupá have been in conflict with the farm that surrounds them and which claims a right to their land.

Alfredo da Cunha, a farmer and former president of the *quilombola* association, makes a point of relating the history of the *quilombo*'s lineage. He speaks slowly, pointedly. He uses short sentences to synthesize major events from the past. With a single word—Africa—he references centuries of the Atlantic slave trade. He curls his right hand tightly into a fist, striking his left palm with small, emphatic punches as he tells his story:

"Africa. To a specific place: Santana. Near Ponta de Pedras. For a while. The slaves were so badly abused. Like animals. I mean, they were scarred. With an iron brand on the arm. Or wherever." And so they fled the sugar plantation in Santana. Alfredo shows me pictures on his cell phone of his visit to the old sugar mill. He gets noticeably choked up.

After fleeing Fazenda Santana, the enslaved would stop at other plantations where many were recaptured, according to Alfredo. Two of them made it as far as Gurupá. "So, long story short, that's what happened. They ran. From Santana to Gurupá. And that's how our community got its name." But their escape was not ultimately successful: the pair was eventually recaptured. Hence the designation they gave themselves: Gurupá, from *gorou o par*, meaning "they went in vain," chosen by the others who would later go on to fully escape slavery, in honor of the two who were recaptured.

The story is undoubtedly tied to history. Nevertheless, the frequency of Alfredo's retellings suggest that, in some way, it still speaks volumes about the challenges and conflicts *quilombolas* are experiencing to this day.

First Female President

The first woman to hold the position of president of the Remanescentes do Quilombo Gurupá community association, Fátima Batista recalls the old conflicts with the farmers. Her voice has reached a point where pain and bravery cannot be told apart. "The late Liberato Magno da Silva Castro was believed to have had a farm in Caroba and another in Boa Vista. This farmer took over our land and set up his own two farms there. But it belonged to us, the Batista family. After that, he got our people moved off the shore here. He put some other families into our community, and he sent others into other places to clear out the area so he could control it."

In the mid-1970s, the *quilombolas* who lived along the branches of the Arari River were driven out by Liberato Castro. Teodoro Lalor de Lima, known as Seu Lalor, was the only one who decided to remain. Eventually, he became president of the *quilombola* association.

There, traditionally, each family unit occupied a particular stream. The streams are part of an area generally considered very fertile, filled with açaí groves cultivated for decades by *quilombolas*. These follow the winding watercourses. During harvest season, the residents transport the açaí berries by boat to be sold in Belém. In the off season, when the land is managed to ensure the trees' continued healthy growth, the main product is the açaí palm itself, although according to the *quilombolas*, this has a lower market value than the berries.

Until the *quilombolas* were removed from the Arari River, the ethnic territory covered both this river and its tributaries as well as the Gurupá River. Since Liberato Castro took over the land, families have had to cluster around Gurupá, where they have been subjected to harassment.

Rosivaldo Correa explains how the output from Liberato Castro's Fazenda São Joaquim Agropecuária depended on rent paid by *quilombolas* for rights to the açaí groves. "The farm primarily raises free-range cattle on extensive fields," he says. "But their biggest source of income was from the açaí groves, which they lease out every year." They charged what they say is "half" the value of açaí harvested in Marajó, but can actually be as high as two-thirds, according to Felipe Moura Palha, a prosecutor with the Federal Public Prosecutor 3rd office for traditional communities.

"In 2002, we created the Remanescentes do Quilombo Gurupá community association, and petitioned INCRA to recognize our territory," Correa recalls. According to him, in 2008, with increasing demand for *quilombola* land, the farmer reacted and the conflict intensified. Only after the process of formalizing the *quilombo* through INCRA had begun could they reclaim the lands from which they had been expelled in the 1970s. The year 2011 finally saw the historic repopulation of the land and streams along the Arari River.

In an interview, Palha said that "the local police are often used to intimidate the *quilombolas*. The company foreman is still there at the farm. He uses the police and his local political influence to persecute and criminalize the *quilombolas*. One of his tactics is to accuse them of stealing açaí. How can a guy be accused of stealing something off the land that belongs to him?" the prosecutor asks.

The Martyrdom of Seu Lalor

A smoldering climate of violence hangs over the Comunidade de Remanescentes do Quilombo Gurupá. Every year, around the summer harvest time, it flares up. In response, the Public Prosecutor's office has taken steps, including sending letters to public authorities and local Cachoeira do Arari government officials "to ensure that the traditional *quilombola* population can enjoy the harvest in accordance with their way of life," Palha says. Açaí has now become a known source of conflict.

"Fear" is a word commonly heard around the *quilombo*. The presence of police and farm agents in the surrounding forest puts the *quilombolas* in the unfortunate position of being observed. Whoever is in the forest can see out, but those outside it cannot see in, and so they are vulnerable. The sense of living under a constant threat of siege occasionally becomes a reality in the form of arrests and attempted murders.

But nothing brought more pain to the community than the killing of Teodoro Lalor de Lima—Seu Lalor, on August 19, 2013. By refusing, back in the 1970s, to leave the banks of the Arari River and its streams—an area that was beginning to be occupied by Liberato Castro—Lalor played an important role in the community. Many years later, sick and elderly, he was arrested and handcuffed to his hospital bed, to the *quilombolas*' great indignation. He also visited Brasília a few times to speak out against what was happening to the community.

Quilombolas still find it hard to accept the explanation given by the Civil Police and reports published by various Pará media regarding the murder of Seu Lalor. "This crime had repercussions, and to this day, we still haven't gotten to the bottom of our leader's death," Fátima Batista says. "They rounded up some guy with a record to charge with the crime, but I believe it was an orchestrated killing".

The alleged perpetrator of the murder was convicted in 2015. The official explanation was that Seu Lalor was at a lover's house and was surprised there by her ex-husband.

The anthropologist Eliana Teles was in close contact with Seu Lalor in the days leading up to his murder. She had just completed her doctorate and was conducting research on the *quilombo*. To her, the whole situation was aimed at demoralizing the inhabitants, at shattering their pride.

For Fátima Batista, the future of the *quilombo* and the safety of its residents depends on regulating the land on which they live. "What we want is the title," she says. "And we want the government to help us get it. If we had the physical title in our hands, this whole scheme of farmers wanting to take over our land would be over. We'd be able to work and get what we want within our own community, our *quilombo*."

INCRA Drags Its Feet

The dispute over the land and its use is the biggest problem facing Quilombo Gurupá. Who got the land, and how, is a central part of that discussion.

In 1989, the Pará state government created an Environmental Protection Area on Marajó Island. Sixteen years later, in 2005, INCRA began the process of recognizing *quilombola* land in the Gurupá community. In 2010, a certification was issued for the territory known as the Comunidade de Remanescentes do Quilombo Gurupá.

But the process stalled when it came to removing squatters and farmers from the lands. Despite the certificate, the *quilombo*'s territory isn't titled by INCRA. "We had meeting after meeting with INCRA, and all they have to say to the people is 'The state has no funds for this, the state can't force them out.' So were basically stuck with documents that aren't worth the paper they're printed on," Fátima Batista says.

The legal dispute with Liberato Castro and his heirs over the territory is a lengthy one. The prosecutor Felipe Palha indicates that it's highly likely the farmer's title was the result of a land grab: a historical practice of corporate farms illegally appropriating public lands in the Amazon and which is often associated with deforestation, the expulsion of local residents, and agrarian violence.

"During this whole process, we found out that the property title, which this farmer, Liberato Castro, offered as proof that the land was legally his, was invalid," Palha says. "It hadn't been properly registered with the public authorities. In all likelihood, this was a land grab. In other words, that area belongs to the union. It's not private. The title Liberato Castro has been waving around is null and void," he concludes.

In a written response to *Amazônia Real*, INCRA confirmed that the "territory pertaining to the Comunidade de Remanescentes do Quilombo Gurupá, in the municipality of Cachoeira do Arari, Marajó region, a Certificate of Self-Determination was issued on June 21, 2010, and was recognized by Presidential Decree on April 1, 2016, with 'a declared social interest for the purposes of expropriation.'" According to the institute, rural properties included in the Gurupá *quilombola* territory are in the phase in which non-*quilombola* occupants are removed.

According to INCRA, there is a lawsuit, filed jointly by the federal agency and Brazil's attorney general, which "aims to declare null and void the property title, followed by the cancellation of the real estate records and registrations of the property known as Imóvel São Joaquim, comprised of the Murutucum Miry, Saparará-Miry, Igarapé da Roça, Santa Roza, Acará, and Gurupá farms, irregularly occupied by the alleged owners, owing to the effects they have on land in the public domain, which includes an area belonging to the Quilombola Territory of Gurupá."

Heir Contests Land-Grabbing Accusation

Consuelo Maria da Silva Castro is Liberato Castro's daughter and heir. She also served as mayor of Ponta de Pedras, a municipality adjacent to Cachoeira do Arari, from 2012 to 2016. She disputes the allegations of land grabbing committed by her family. "That land there doesn't just belong to my father," she says. "It's in my father's name because he was the executor and eldest son. But originally it belonged to my grandmother, who kept it in the family. It's four children's inheritance. Land that was bought by the crown, right there at the mouth of the river, at the entrance to the Arari River."

According to Consuelo, no *quilombo* ever existed there. "Does the government want to take what you've got and give it to those who don't? So would it reimburse us for the cattle there? And for the improvements we made to the land? The land that you're saying isn't even ours?" speculates the former mayor, now Director of Agricultural Development at the Ministry of Fisheries and Aquaculture in the state of Pará.

On December 18, 2018, the attorney general filed a basic injunction requesting that the property title be declared null and void, and that real estate records and orders of reintegration of possession be cancelled. The lawsuit has yet to be heard by the Federal Court. In short, if it's deemed to be valid, Liberato Castro and his heirs "wouldn't be entitled to compensation, because their possession of the land was done in bad faith," Palha says. "In this process of removing current occupants, there wouldn't even be compensation for Liberato Castro's farm."

Bargaining by Public Agents

When it comes to the phenomenon of rice farmers popping up everywhere, from Roraima to Marajó, Palha points to political bargains available to public officials that enable farmers to continue working in the area. "Authorities in Pará made agreements to allow rice farmers to come to Marajó Island," he said.

Palha went on to say that the Public Prosecutor's office warned farmers that *quilombola* populations were already living in the area and that prior consultation was necessary before any land was tilled. The Environmental Impact Study would also have to be taken into account. "None of this was done," he said. "They pushed everything through a simplified licensing process in order to kickstart farming in Marajó."

Based on his experience with similar cases involving palm oil in eastern Pará, the prosecutor drew comparisons with other incidents of monocropping implemented in the Amazon. "We alerted the local authorities, letting them know it was going to happen. And it did. The conflict between rice farmers and traditional communities in Marajó is just another chapter in the long history of people exploiting the rainforest without regard for anything. Not even for the people already living there," he said.

Palha went on to warn that, while the farm is not technically within the *quilombolas'* territory, its activities *are* affecting the territory. "The community certainly isn't benefitting from silt and pollution building up in their streams." He also reflects, more broadly, that "the greatest mistake of the economic development in the Amazon, and especially in Pará, is that they don't care about the fact that people actually live there."

A Different Look for Marajó

Eliana Teles, a researcher with a long history of working in Marajó, laments the transformation of the archipelago's terrain. "The countryside, which European travelers marveled over when they passed through in the seventeenth and eighteenth centuries . . . that vibrant landscape they described is now dominated by agribusiness: rice in the Arari watershed, which includes part of Salvaterra, while further to the east, the northwest part of the region is being covered in soy."

Despite the lack of specific studies, mathematics professor Rosivaldo Correa, who lives within the Quilombo confirms what, in the view of those feeling the rice fields' impact on a daily basis, has become obvious. "You don't need to be an expert to know that we're bearing the brunt of this, as much in the rivers as on land," he says, boiling it all down. "There's nothing good for us on the horizon."

DAYS AND NIGHTS in an Indigenous village can be tedious. Most of the day revolves around activities which require a certain skill set, leaving someone like me, born and raised in an urban environment, unable to contribute. I try, but I'm not much of a hunter or fisherman, and my ability at clearing the manioc fields was so lacking that the Tupinambá—a people with whom I spent most of my time in the Amazon and with whom I'm writing my doctoral thesis—definitely preferred that I keep out of their way.

The fact is there isn't an important interview every day. Often, my primary goal of the day is "just" seeking refuge from the sun. These days are repeated with impressive regularity, and are especially slow and weighty.

When the sun sets, I often go out with Josi, one of *cacica* Estevina's nephews, for a canoe ride. Josi recently turned eighteen, and is starting a physical education course at a private school in Santarém, so he divides his time between the village and the city. So when he is around, we go out on the water. When he isn't, I stay in.

I took a small canoe this time, smaller than the one I normally used with Josi. It took me a while to figure out how to balance it. Only after a disastrous twenty minutes of failing to navigate myself out of the smaller watercourse into the larger Amorim stream did I realize I was attempting to paddle backwards. Happy to have figured this out, and happier still that, thanks to the dense undergrowth, nobody in the village had noticed my predicament, I decided, confidently, to head out to the first bend in the stream.

Then, believing I had finally mastered the vessel, I thought I could calmly proceed to the second bend. As I approached, in the distance I saw a black animal swimming in the water.

Without binoculars, I could only barely make it out, but my excitement was such that I decided to venture closer. It looked like an *ariranha*, a giant river otter. I'd seen one earlier on the bank, and was fascinated by its shiny black fur. I naively decide to paddle faster in order to reach it.

The animal was swimming from left to right. The Amorim stream is a winding one, and its lush borders alternate between flooded forest and strips of land at the entrance to the villages. These flooded areas exist only during the rainy season, and are marked by twisting trees with aerial roots through which you can navigate a canoe to fish, as well as be surprised by the occasional snake.

I was afraid the animal would duck into the labyrinthine tangle of trees and roots and I'd lose sight of it. As I grew closer, I could see that it wasn't an otter at all: there was a huge head above the water, and a tail poking up in the back. A bull, I thought to myself. But then again, I wondered, "What's a bull doing here, in the middle of the rainforest, swimming from one bank to another?" After a few more strokes, I was able to discern a pair of pointed ears, like those of a cat.

It was a jaguar.

More precisely, a black panther, which is simply a jaguar with an excess of black pigmentation.

I had seen a jaguar.

But had it seen me?

A game of fleeting glimpses so uncertain that I have to wonder whether "game" is the right word for it.

That uncertainty may well be why panic suddenly overcame me.

I rowed on, constantly looking behind me, afraid the jaguar was on my tail and ready to capsize my canoe at any moment. I could almost hear the *dun-dun, dun-dun* music that precedes a shark attack in *Jaws*.

All my difficulty paddling the canoe vanished. If I took forty minutes to get to the second bend in the creek, I made it back to the village in ten. I arrived breathless, while at the same time thrilled by what I had just witnessed. I told everyone what I'd seen, and none of them had any doubts about my account. "It was definitely a jaguar," the Tupinambá nodded, one by one. As they usually do, everyone had fun with the story. As spirited as ever and playfully feigning fearlessness, Seu Pedrinho added, "If it'd been me, I'd have rowed right over its head." I'm sure that the next time I come to visit, my story will be the source of great entertainment.

The strangeness, the otherness of being in a place as different and unique as a Tupinambá village in the middle of the Amazon rainforest suddenly becomes relative. In a matter of days, we can succumb to routine, we can forget that we're surrounded by a jungle where it's entirely possible to have a singular encounter with something as extraordinary as a black panther crossing a stream.

The *Kumuã* of the Upper Rio Negro and the Decolonization of Indigenous Bodies

The remote Base São José II, a medical clinic located in the Special Indigenous Sanitary District (DSEI) of São Gabriel da Cachoeira, has gone without doctors since Cuba revoked its partnership with the Brazilian government in December 2018. This was a riposte to the recently elected president Jair Bolsonaro, who resented the fortuitous help of Cuban medical professionals. The clinic provides health services to the local Indigenous population, and nurses occasionally travel to even more remote villages where not even radio communication works. Located on the Middle Tiquié River and surrounded by the dense Amazon rainforest, it is about two days' journey by motorboat from São Gabriel da Cachoeira, near the border with Colombia.

A schedule hanging on a wall at the clinic indicates an intense agenda of work and service for the villages. Yet this effort is subject to criticism. "This health care that comes in from the outside is replacing Indigenous knowledge," asserts Domingos Borges Barreto, a Tukano who lives in São Gabriel da Cachoeira. "This is an Indigenous Territory, but they don't care about what the Indigenous people know. Dipyrone is replacing the *pajé*," he continues, referring to the complex system of caring for and healing the body practiced by the Indigenous peoples of the Upper Rio Negro, who, today, center themselves around the *kumu*: a figure defined by whites under the generic term *pajé*, or shaman.

João Paulo Lima Barreto is Tukano and is a doctoral student in anthropology at the Center for the Study of the Indigenous Amazon (NEAI), at the Federal University of Amazonas. For him, the *kumu* has the ability to summon healing and protective properties. The kumu has a precise understanding of sickness and health, of how to constitute and care for the body through *bahsese* (shamanic therapy), *bahsamori* (songs and rituals), and *kihti* (the stories told by the Tukano people).

"He is the keeper of the body's formulas," João Paulo says, describing the *kumu* as a central figure. In this researcher's view, the totality of Indigenous knowledge is "as complex as that of science, which denies, discards, and doesn't understand it. It's a very complicated system that was messed up by white people," he adds.

There is an entire branch of the Brazilian government structured towards Indigenous wellness. Native people are expected to have differentiated access to health care though the Special Secretariat for Indigenous Health (SESAI), which operates under the Ministry of Health. The Special Indigenous Sanitary Districts, which report to the federal government, can operate in one or across several of Brazil's Indigenous Territories and are able to enter into partnerships with state, local, and nongovernmental organizations.

But for Lucila Gonçalves, a psychologist and researcher in the field of Indigenous health, "The Indigenous peoples' knowledge is not often taken into account in an equal, balanced way. Technically there's a proposal for integration, but their wisdom and experience ends up being disqualified in favor of biomedicine." In the Xingu Indigenous Territory, where Lucila has spent the last few years doing research for her PhD, there is a working proposal for integration, though it is far from effectively implemented. Lucila describes what happened to Mapulu, an important midwife and shaman of Kamaiurá heritage who lived in Canarana, a municipality outside the Xingu territory. During a delivery in which she participated, the hospital's doctor wouldn't allow Mapulu to enter the room and perform her ceremonial rituals, which involve blowing on the patient. She had to physically remove the patient from the hospital in order to perform the ceremony while the doctor protested. When the patient's condition improved, the doctor returned to apologize.

It is against this backdrop, in which Indigenous knowledge is relegated to the second tier or treated as mere spiritual beliefs, that important experiments validating Indigenous knowledge come into focus. Hamyla Elizabeth da Silva Trindade is a nurse and Indigenous Baré woman who's partly responsible for the Indigenous Health Center (CASAI) in São Gabriel da Cachoeira. According to a 2018 report, the facility treats an average of ninety-six people per month, most of them for pneumonia, diarrhea, malaria, and suspected tuberculosis. "At the CASAI, there are Indigenous people every day asking for a shaman to perform the shamanic therapies and rituals. We're constantly dealing with holy water and tobacco used as incense. We work with this relationship between traditional and Western medicine," Hamyla says, stressing this last point.

João Paulo Lima Barreto, however, wants to go even further. "The Indigenous people are getting addicted to medications, and forgetting our own ways of healing," he says. This is part of the knowledge that João Paulo brought to Manaus when he created the Bahserikowi'i Indigenous Medicine Center in June 2017, where the *kumuã* (plural of *kumu*) from the Upper Rio Negro treat both Indigenous and non-Indigenous people alike.

In addition, as an experienced pilot, he works with his father, *kumu* Ovídio, attending to sick Indigenous people at the CASAI in Manaus. "This is a partnership between the Bahserikowi'i center and the Manaus CASAI. We bring the human capital and they provide infrastructure and organization."

I followed João Paulo's return to his native village after fifteen years studying in Manaus. Originally named Uhremiripa, meaning "Warbler Rapids," before the arrival of Salesian missionaries, and today known as the community of São Domingos Sávio, the village is extremely difficult to reach. By motorboat, it takes two days to go up the Tiquié Riverfrom the Village to the Colombian border, with two large waterfalls along the way.

Whiling away the long hours on the boat from São Gabriel da Cachoeira to São Domingos, and sheltering ourselves as best we could from the scorching sun and freezing rain, we began to glimpse the lives of people struggling to preserve Indigenous ways of understanding and dealing with the world. Having faced persecution by the Roman Catholic Church in the early twentieth century, and with the current state health-care system poorly equipped to deal with Indigenous knowledge and practices, the Indigenous people's struggle to transmit this knowledge despite the harsh life of the villages and the prejudice they suffer in the town of São Gabriel gave me much pause for thought.

Roughly four out of five of São Gabriel da Cachoeira's forty-five thousand residents are Indigenous, the largest proportion of any municipality in Brazil. Members of the Arapaso, Baniwa, Barasana, Baré, Desana, Hupda, Karapanã, Kubeo, Kuripako, Makuna, Miriti-Tapuya, Nadöb, Pira-tapuya, Siriano, Tariana, Tukano, Tuyuka, Wanana, Werekena, and Yanomami ethnic groups make the city a truly multicultural territory. You can hear different languages spoken on every street corner. Diversity is so ingrained that Municipal Law 145, enacted on November 22, 2002, recognized Nheengatu, Tukano, and Baniwa as the city's three official languages.

Inspired by that civic initiative, João Paulo is looking into the possibility of drafting a state law recognizing the *kumuã* and other shamans from different Amazon populations as specialists able to work on diagnosing illnesses and prescribing curative measures alongside doctors who practice Western medicine.

A Dangerous World

For the Tukano, the world requires constant mediation between the *kumuã* and the *Wai-Mahsã*, the guardians of places. Given that everything in the world has a guardian that's responsible for it, there needs to be mediation: from consuming food to entering the forest and fishing, from childbirth to dealing with children's growing up and the body's development. The *Wai-Mahsã* are the ones who possess the knowledge and understanding of the rituals and *bahsese* therapies; therefore, communications via the *kumuã* are fundamental for access to that knowledge. The body, which is in a state of constant formation, requires its own care, involving food, protection, and practices like *bahsese* performed by experts.

Communication between the *Wai-Mahsã* and the experts requires a strict ceremony centered around preparing the body by ingesting substances such as the juice of certain vines and parica, a snuff with hallucinogenic properties. This preparation is completed before large events, and as a part of it, the *kumuã* are forbidden from eating certain foods, such as game meat and large, fatty fish. If these requirements aren't met, the *Wai-Mahsã* can become angry.

Traditionally, there are three types of expert practitioners among the Tukano and a few other Indigenous groups in the Upper Rio Negro who all work together to treat the body. The *yaí* is the one with the ability to diagnose diseases; the *kumu* is responsible for caring for the patient after they have been diagnosed by the *yaí* through *bahsese* and the use of medicinal plants; the *bayá* is an expert who leads the great ceremonies and is also responsible for the shamanic rituals. According to Indigenous beliefs, the dialogue between these experts and the invisible beings is what sustains the forces of the cosmos and maintains the environmental balance in the rainforest.

The Salesian missionaries, who founded their center in São Gabriel da Cachoeira in 1916 before spreading out along the Uaupés, Tiquié, and other rivers in the borderlands between Brazil, Colombia, and Venezuela, did not look favorably upon this Indigenous knowledge. Their missionary work took hold amid the decline of the rubber industry in the 1920s. In a way, the colonial focus shifted from controlling the body in order to generate a workforce to controlling the soul in order to generate believers. Targeted in the name of "reclaiming the poor savages"—the exact language used in the 1917 *Salesian Bulletin*—the *kumuã*, responsible for the formation of Indigenous bodies, began to be persecuted.

"Our experts were compared to witches," says João Paulo. "Our knowledge was categorized as profane. We were demonized and persecuted." According to the Indigenous anthropologist, the *kumuã* and *bayá* have become scarce, while the *yaí* have now all but disappeared. The communal longhouses were destroyed and replaced with homes designed for single families. Salesian Catholics believed the longhouses were sites for incestuous orgies, and considered the ceremonies and healing rituals to be satanic. They ignored marriage traditions such as the one indicating Tukano men should marry Tuyuka women and gain knowledge about *bahsese* and medicinal plants from their in-laws.

The Salesians' "civilizing" process consisted of four stages, which were enumerated in the 1930 *Salesian Bulletin*: "First, abandon the longhouse, a place which, by its very nature, begets corruption, so that each one may live in his own home; second, desist with the recurrent orgies and inevitable drunkenness; third, realize the marriage without the violent abduction of the wife and instead by mutual agreement; and fourth, participate in Sunday Mass."

"Many *kumuã* died from the sadness of not being able to practice their craft," João Paulo explains. "My grandfather was nearly one of them. For him, practicing his craft was vital to his existence." According to João Paulo, his grandfather's confiscated tools and instruments are now on display at the Museu do Índio in Manaus. The remaining *kumuã* are destined to vanish due to the combined effects of missionaries' and the nonreligious whites' education systems, which bring Indigenous people out of the rainforest and into the cities, only to relegate their knowledge to a mere curiosity. João Paulo criticizes anthropology itself, which continues to view *bahsese* as a kind of religious ritual, while to him the challenge is more about "bringing our own Indigenous concepts to the debate, and thus escaping from this jargon." This is why he prefers to use expressions like "therapeutic techniques" and "experts."

Durvalino Moura Fernandes, a *kumu* of the Desano people (his name, in Desano, is Kisibi) has lived in São Gabriel da

Cachoeira with his wife, Judith, since 2001. He says that his father was a great *kumu*, and from him he learned to perform *bahsese*, the important therapies that form and protect people. "You will stand in my place, and you will learn how to give the therapy," his father told him. For Durvalino, "The education provided by white culture is putting an end to our therapies." City life makes it very difficult for the *kumuã* to share knowledge with one another, so he is working with other *kumu* to create a school, a place for exchanging experiences, in a village yet to be determined. He is skeptical of the *kumuã* who are proliferating throughout the city without undergoing the same, rigorous training.

Persecution by the Catholic Church culminated in eliminating the production of parica, today found mainly among the Indigenous people of the Colombian rainforest. Judith Fernandes Sarmiento, whose given name in Tukano is Yuhsio (a mythical heroine who aligns a woman's processing of knowledge), is the granddaughter of a powerful *kumu*. Her father couldn't learn *bahsese* techniques from his own father, who had been raised as an altar boy and worked as a cleaner and tailor. He only came to learn *bahsese* when Judith married Durvalino and her father-in-law began teaching him.

Judith says that, these days, her husband takes great care of the Franciscan nuns. "They want their bodies protected so they don't catch any of the diseases around here, so he cleanses them with fragrances and lotions." In the past, Durvalino says, "Priests called the *kumu* the devil. Nowadays, they're more understanding." This *kumu* has a playful way about him, and he laughingly repeats the same expression—"and so, consequently"—which itself is a commentary on the very topic we're dealing with and the consequences that past persecutions have to this day.

"Well, Fábio, we're here at the Padres' Headquarters," João Paulo said as we disembarked in what was once the Salesian mission in Pari-Cachoeira, where his family now lives. São Domingos Sávio, where he was born, is about half an hour upriver by motorboat (it's a day trip if you're paddling), towards Colombia. Because of the school, Pari-Cachoeira continues to exert a powerful attraction over the Indigenous people, especially the Tukano, who go to the site of the old mission in search of better education for their children.

In the past, the Church had "captains" in every village. "When the captain learned about a practicing *kumu*, he would hunt him down and order everything to be seized," João Paulo says. "They were also exerting psychological and economic pressure by not selling matches, soap, clothes, or tobacco to communities with active *kumuã*." They forced the Indigenous people to paddle their canoes for days in order to attend special celebrations like Easter and Christmas.

I spoke with one of the priests responsible for the São João Bosco parish, where the boarding school used to be. Joãonilton Lemos Castanho is one of the Tariana people, from Taraquá, at the head of the Tiquié River, and has been in Pari-Cachoeira for the past year and a half. "I look at this history from an optimistic point of view," the priest says. "These communities are what they are today thanks to the Salesians." He considers himself a product of this endeavor, and speaks proudly of the order, which managed to establish itself in the Upper Rio Negro area where the Jesuits had previously failed. I then ask him about the way the Church handled the Indigenous peoples' customs, specifically the curative practices of the *kumuã*, who were persecuted.

"At that time, there was a clash between two realities, two cultures. The missionaries arrived from Europe and imposed their beliefs. In a sense, it represented the loss of our own culture: the dances, the nakedness. It was a great loss," the priest admits.

João Paulo remembers life in Pari-Cachoeira in great detail. He was sent there aged nine, risking his chances of becoming an expert practitioner of Indigenous medicine, whether as a *yaí*, a *kumu*, or a *bayá*. All three require specific, meticulous training, which could then have been passed on to many of his siblings and cousins. With a forlorn note to his voice, he recalls how his life changed when he departed the village for a boarding school with 150 other children, governed by a stern, religious discipline defined by teaching and hard work. "My daily schedule was to wake up, eat, pray, study, go out to work in the fields, and go to sleep." Everything took place under the watchful supervision of the Salesians, who forbade the Indigenous children from ever speaking Tukano. "Anyone who got caught speaking it had to wear a sign with a picture of a donkey on it," he says. The intent was to transform the Indigenous boys into civilized, European men through baptism, work, and discipline.

While in Pari-Cachoeira, João Paulo earned a scholarship to study extraction techniques in Manaus, from a mining company interested in the region. After graduating, he returned to Pari-Cachoeira to teach at the same boarding school he had attended. He went on to join the priesthood, but then returned to Manaus where he began studying law and definitively abandoned his religious life. Today, he considers himself a nonpracticing Christian. Taking advantage of a quota program, he enrolled in the Amazonas State University, embarking on a period of intense involvement with the Indigenous movement.

João Paulo had hoped to find some sort of dialogue between the prelaw program and the Tukano curriculum, a way to reflect on Indigenous concepts and what's known as "customary law," or the legal premises that arise from a given society's customs. But the prelaw program wasn't open to such interdisciplinary discussions, so he backed out and decided to try his luck with the Department of Philosophy instead. His proposal for a thesis on Indigenous philosophy was promptly rejected by the faculty, who believed there was no standardized bibliography on which the student could base his research. In the end it was anthropology, thanks to the man who would become his advisor and friend, Professor Gilton Mendes dos Santos, where João Paulo found an environment in which he could bring together all the different systems of knowledge he had been employing in his daily life, from the day he was shipped off to boarding school in Pari-Cachoeira.

João Paulo's view of the Church, his trajectory, and the institutions through which he passed, is not simply that a culture was destroyed and everything lost. When he and his brother José Maria revisited the boarding school, he remarked that he saw all of it as an instrument for transformation. "I once thought this was all about loss, but now I don't believe it is," he said. "It is possible to have an understanding with the *Wai-Mahsã*, because they exist on a separate plane, not the plane of the loss." With expert practitioners starting to train again, using isolation, teachings, food, and certain substances for internal cleansing and opening up the body, João Paulo believes it is possible to connect with the *Wai-Mahsã* once again and recover any knowledge "forgotten" in this worldly plane.

Part of João Paulo's realization happened during the trip to Alto Rio Tiquié when we stopped for lunch in a small Tukano community at the foot of the Serra da Mucura. There, a respected *kumu* known as Ahkuto told an elaborate story about the origins of the mountains behind the village as well as the emergence of diseases and the curative therapies associated with them. Afterwards, he explained that the story didn't exist in the words he spoke. That it had taken place all on its own, and was written on the rocks, on the mountain, in the rivers and waterways. For the Tukano, knowledge of *bahsese* and creation narratives seems to be embedded in the very landscape itself.

The Jararaca's Bite

The story of the Bahserikowi'i Indigenous Medicine Center begins with a traumatic event for the family of João Paulo Lima Barreto, founder of the project. Despite the daily contact we had with his niece, Luciene Lima Barreto, in Pari-Cachoeira and in the São Domingos community, she refused to talk about the accident that nearly took her life. She did, however, agree to let her father, José Maria Barreto (also known in Tukano as Ahkuto), tell us this story.

One afternoon in December 2009, while collecting shrimp in the São Domingos stream, Luciene was bitten on the foot by a highly venomous pit viper known as a *jararaca*. The eleven-year-old was taken to Pari-Cachoeira, where she was given an antivenom serum provided by a remote military platoon base and began treatments using traditional Tukano remedies. Amid fear that her condition might worsen, Luciene was transferred to São Gabriel da Cachoeira, a day away by motorboat. But, according to José Maria, when they reached the city, things got worse "due to the presence of menstruating women." Like other Indigenous people, the Tukano see menstruation and blood flow as potentially dangerous when the order of the world is thrown into disarray. This danger requires special treatment, and oftentimes the afflicted person is placed in quarantine in order for their body to restore its equilibrium.

Luciene arrived in São Gabriel on the same day as a young member of the Baniwa people who also had a snake bite. He died the next day. José Maria could tell that the doctors were growing desperate when Luciene was sent to Manaus, where they hoped she would receive better treatment. They checked in to the emergency room at the Hospital Dr. João Lúcio Pereira Machado; José Maria stayed there in the waiting room for hours while his daughter was in treatment. When she woke, Luciene exclaimed: "They're going to cut off my whole foot!" She described the recommended medical procedures, and began to plead: "I don't want to live anymore. Let me die, daddy. I don't want to live without a foot!"

According to José Maria, the attending doctors believed that, if they didn't amputate the foot filled with jararaca venom, Luciene would be dead within seventy-two hours. However, the *kumuã* who examined her arrived at a different diagnosis. Seu Ovídio, father of José Maria and João Paulo Lima Barreto, assured them that, through *bahsese* and traditional remedies, Luciene would soon be on the path to recovery.

Hospital doctors wouldn't allow the *kumuã* anywhere near the girl. They said that they, who had spent eight years in medical school, were the only ones allowed to be there. "We wanted to get her out of there, but the doctors wouldn't let us," José Maria said. "They called me an Indian, said I was from the jungle, and if I took her she would die right out there in the street." He and Seu Ovídio asked why pastors and priests were allowed to visit patients, but not a shaman. Feeling upset, offended, and disrespected, the Barreto family called the Public Prosecutor's office and filed a motion that prevented the hospital from amputating Luciene's foot and allowed them to take her home. After four days in legal and medical limbo, she was finally discharged. During that time, Seu Ovídio and João Paulo were able to "smuggle" some *bahsese* water into the hospital. "That's what gave her strength," José Maria assured me.

The whole story was played out in the press. While Luciene was receiving treatment at an outpatient facility for the Indigenous people of the Upper Rio Negro region, back in Manaus, Dr. Remerson Monteiro of the Getúlio Vargas university hospital, affiliated with the Federal University of Amazonas, sought out her relatives. "He was more understanding, and allowed our shaman and his medicines to participate," José Maria recalls. In addition to Seu Ovídio, two other Tukano *kumuã* participated in the healing process, along with the hospital doctors. According to Elaíze Farias, a reporter who at the time was covering the story for the newspaper *A Crítica* and who is also a cofounder of the *Amazônia Real* news agency, the doctors themselves were impressed by the improvements in Luciene's clinical condition. When she first checked in to the university hospital, it was estimated that she would be in treatment there for seven months. In fact, Luciene was released after just six weeks. To this day, she still has difficulty walking, and has an enormous scar on her lower shin.

Ever since then, João Paulo Lima Barreto has dedicated himself to coming up with and proposing other opportunities for communication and cooperation between the complex system of Indigenous beliefs and the canon of Western medicine.

"Life is just awful for Indigenous people in the city," reflects Domingos Borges Barreto, one of João Paulo's relatives. "I worked for FUNAI for ten years, so I know what it's like. They're on the verge of starvation. Everything is in short supply, from food to dignity. It's a den of all the worst things: violence, racism, discrimination." One of the biggest problems facing São Gabriel da Cachoeira's Indigenous population is the suicide rate, currently among the highest in Brazil.

Domingos says he actively participated in the Indigenous movement, something which often conflicted with his role as a public servant. "First and foremost, I'm Indian. The problem was, I spoke up a lot," he recalls. For him, there were three main reasons that drove the Indigenous people to leave their village homes and venture into the city, a phenomenon he believes has increased over the past thirty years: education for their children, sophisticated health care, and fractures within their own communities.

At a parent-teacher conference, Domingos asked whether there was a place for traditional beliefs in the school's curriculum, and several Indigenous parents complained: "Oh no, here he goes again, always talking about traditions, about *bahsese* . . ." As he puts it, "Practically everything that's local is invisible. Ignored. Everything we try to teach at home gets eliminated by the school." He believes that the handling of food in the villages has changed, that the elders no longer pass on all their knowledge to the younger generation, which seems to think that everything coming in from outside the community is better and will solve all their problems. "There's no such thing as a poor, unequal Indian," he says. "There's culture, there's land, there's autonomy. Medicine, knowledge, food . . . the elders had these things." Domingos is concerned about the way in which Indigenous traditions should be taught: not as a theory, as is the case currently, but on a daily basis, with the older generations spending time with younger people. "In the classroom, that sort of thing can be a bit weird," he concludes.

When we arrived in São Gabriel, we were able to witness a ritualistic Tuyuka festival, which was part of the opening ceremony to a three-day council organized by the Tuyuka Indigenous Association of São Gabriel da Cachoeira. Cipriano Marques Lima, president of the association and himself recognized as a great *kumu*, told us, in the midst of dances, songs, and the use of ceremonial substances such as *caxiri* (fermented manioc) and parica, that the association was created with the intent of reviving ritual festivals and healing practices.

A few days later we returned to the association's office, which is also where a large nuclear family lives. They have been moving to the city gradually over the past three decades, coming from the Colombian border. The development of *kumuã* and the transmission of Indigenous knowledge has been the object of constant reflection in the city. "Knowledge isn't passed down simply by getting together," asserts Angelina Marques Lima, of the Tuyuka people. "It's not that the *kumu* won't tell you. He will, but only as a story. It's through *bahsese* that the mind is opened up to receiving this knowledge." Also central to the process is *carpi*, a vine from which another type of snuff is made. The *kumu* use it "for the person to be able to gain more knowledge," Angelina says.

In the taxi we took right after the festival, I tried talking with the driver about how he perceives Indigenous people in the city. A white man, he didn't hesitate to answer: "That firewater is strong, right? They're all drunks." When it comes to the Indigenous way of life, the violence and prejudice that exists today is not unrelated to the worldview held by missionaries from the early twentieth century: judgements are made about the Indigenous ritual life based on European standards.

Decolonizing Health

In mid-March 2019, I attended a talk given by João Paulo at the CASAI hospital in Manaus, along with Indigenous people from all across the state of Amazonas. *Kumu* Ovídio was also there, in a special room just for him, where he could diagnose patients and update their medical records. His prescriptions include performing *bahsese* and fumigation or otherwise using specific medicinal plants, along with treatments proposed by doctors trained in Western medicine. During the conference, the suggestion of sharing healing techniques and knowledge of medicinal plants among different peoples was well received. The group's basic belief is that the health-care system will gradually open up to Indigenous healing techniques. In fact, this was already happening in Brazilian medicine, which now includes acupuncture, as one of the white nurses participating in the conference pointed out.

The struggle to decolonize Indigenous health is winning on another front as well. Earlier that month, in São Domingos Sávio, on the Upper Tiquié River, João Paulo—speaking mainly in his native Tukano language, which I was trying with great interest to follow, fishing for a word or two in Portuguese—told me excitedly about a meeting among his relatives.

It was then that they decided to establish an Indigenous biovegetal research laboratory. The next steps will include a meeting between *kumuã* and others well versed in medicinal plants, and starting to produce medicines that take into account a greater understanding of the rainforest. The proposal includes plans to have them on the market in São Gabriel da Cachoeira, Manaus, and potentially major cities in the southeast.

Colonization, understood as a long-lasting and violent political process, seems to be centered around the body. Even when it comes to religious catechisms supposedly directed at the soul, it is the physical body that emerges as the focal point for exercising power and discipline, perhaps as a way of gaining access to the soul. Bodies are considered objects that are available to perform the work imposed upon them. This belief runs contrary to Indigenous views, the focus of which is directed more towards the constant process of formation, construction, and care, based on techniques such as *bahsese*. For the colonization process to be able to target neglected or overlooked bodies, bodies for which traditional processes of formation and growth were perfectly adequate, they had to be emptied, eviscerated, with an eye toward making them vulnerable and available to a political and economic regime that exists solely to impose an image of itself upon the other, solely as a form of domination: domination of the other, of nature, and of the body itself. If it's up to João Paulo Lima Barreto, his family, and the *kumuã* of the Upper Rio Negro region, the continuation of Indigenous healing and care of the body is far from over. It's a true bodily rebellion.

I COVERED THE FREE LAND CAMP on two separate occasions, in 2018 and 2019.

On both occasions, it was as exhausting as it was exciting. Marching up and down the Ministries Esplanade. Entering Congress along with hundreds of Indigenous people with painted faces and grass skirts, barefoot and bare chested. Wading into the fountain in front of the Ministry of Justice to get the perfect shot of Indigenous people bathing. Keeping an eye on movements by the police, wary of an attack by the shock troops or mounted officers, standing alongside Indigenous families from across the country.

The look of hatred and contempt in the eyes of the officers leaves no doubt as to the message they want to convey: Indigenous people are not welcome here. Elected officials who were supposed to serve them use a different strategy to gain the same objective. They just ignore the protestors' presence. They simply don't acknowledge them. And the excuses are always the same: either they've no schedule time, or they're out of the country.

In *Os Involuntários da Pátria* ("Involuntary Citizens"), a public lecture presented in downtown Rio de Janeiro that was later published and widely circulated, Brazilian anthropologist Eduardo Viveiros de Castro describes the Free Land Camp:

> And they invade, occupy, and reinvent the Three Powers Plaza in Brasília. It is only fair that the invaded ones retake the headquarters of the invaders. A symbolic guerrilla operation, to be sure, though one that pales in comparison to the massive, real (though also symbolic) war being waged by the invaders.

In 2019, I attempted to cover one of the sessions in the Chamber of Deputies. That was when everything seemed to change. The Bolsonaro administration proudly paraded explicitly anti-Indigenous measures and speeches. They were clearly talking about genocide. The hatred was veiled no more. Any sort of decorum, however cynical it might have been, had now been destroyed. The floodgates were opened on the day Bolsonaro, still a federal representative during the impeachment of President Dilma Rousseff, praised the military leaders who tortured Rousseff and countless other liberal leaders during Brazil's dictatorship. After that point—when a state representative pays homage to a state criminal—it became a free-for-all. The fragile ethical dam that had upheld some semblance of mutual respectability had been shattered. Walking through the halls of Congress, it occurred to me that there was something pornographic about the Bolsonaro administration: everything about it had become explicit. Much to the surprise of those who believed in civilization and culture, this attitude of "anything goes," this brazen, "there, I've said it" logic, attracted supporters.

Another watershed event was the election of an Indigenous congresswoman, Joenia Wapishana, the first in the history of Brazil. That changed everything. It inspired hope. A singular voice in a sea of barbarism.

Unfortunately, I was not able to enter the session. I think it was debating whether to bring the demarcation of Indigenous lands before the Ministry of Justice. But I can't be sure. I remained outside, along with hundreds of Indigenous people and their supporters, all decked out in full Native regalia.

I stepped away for a minute to use the restroom. Inside, Pataxó Indigenous from southern Bahia were dropping their skirts to use the urinals. It must have been an unusual sight to the attendant, who was much more accustomed to seeing men dressed in suits and ties. With a stutter, he asked the Indigenous people who they were, where they came from, and what they were calling for. They answered him, a bit begrudgingly, in low, suspicious voices, as they adjusted their skirts before leaving.

The restroom attendant couldn't contain himself in the face of the Pataxós' curt reply. "You're here because of the l-l-l-land, aren't you?" he asked with a wry grin. "You need to occupy it. . . . White people are such shameless bastards!"

Between the Festival and the Fight: The Life of the First Indigenous Person in Brazil to Die from COVID-19

She died on March 19, 2020. The wake went on until dawn. Many people, including the elderly, came to spend that night watching over the body of Dona Lusia dos Santos Lobato. She was eighty-seven. The Indigenous leader, whose life story is inextricably linked to the struggle for the rights and recognition of the Borari people, was beloved in the village of Alter do Chão, near Santarém in western Pará.

Confirmation by the Pará State Department of Public Health that Dona Lusia had died from COVID-19 generated trepidation and fear. Relatives and others who'd been in close contact with her were quarantined, but this also generated a sense of mistrust among family members, who were reluctant to believe her death was the result of the new coronavirus. Dona Lusia was the first Indigenous person to succumb to the disease in Brazil. Because she didn't live in a village recognized by FUNAI, her death is not included among the statistics collected by the Ministry of Health.

Dona Lusia was born in an unusual way. Alter do Chão is located along the banks of the Tapajós River; it's known for its beautiful lakes and beaches, which have made it one of the most well-known, picturesque places in the Amazon region. Local families lived primarily on fishing, hunting, and clearing land for cultivation until the mid-1970s, when a land route connecting the village with the urban area of Santarém was opened.

During the Amazonian summer, which runs from August to October, the Borari people, along with others who live in the village, take advantage of the dry season to move around. They visit family in nearby communities or cities, or travel to lowland areas to plant crops where lower river levels have exposed particularly fertile soil. It was during one of these seasonal trips that Dona Lusia was born: in a canoe, on the way to Urucurituba, in Amazonas state, where her mother was going to visit relatives.

"Despite being a child of the waters, my mother didn't know how to swim," recalls Ludinea Lobato Gonçalves Dias, better known as Neca Borari, one of Dona Lusia's seven daughters, who is also an important Indigenous *cacica* and leader in Alter do Chão. For Neca, Dona Lusia is a source of inspiration.

"I praise God that my mother gave me a lot of strength to be an Indigenous person," she says. Then, her voice trembling with emotion, she recalls Dona Lusia's advice: "Just be careful, because lots of leaders end up getting killed, and I don't want to see your body turn up somewhere. But always go with strength.

"Alter do Chão has a history of being a matriarchal village. If you did a survey here, you'd see that 70 percent of households are run by women," Neca explains. In fact, Dona Lusia never married. According to her daughter, "She never let herself be subjugated by a man. She raised us all on her own."

The Borari people live in two different locations, both in the Lower Tapajós River Basin. The Borari/Alter do Chão territory, which is currently in the process of being recognized by the National Indian Foundation, consists of four villages: Curucuruí, Caranã, São Raimundo, and Alter do Chão. The other territory is the Maró Indigenous Land, which has already been identified and demarcated by FUNAI. Besides the Borari, the Indigenous Arapiuns people live there as well, sharing the territory between the municipalities of Santarém and Parintins.

According to Neca Borari, in the early 1970s, the opening of the road to Santarém created an unexpected situation for local residents. "Tourism brought something we weren't prepared for: real estate speculation. That was the end of it. After that, it was all fight, fight, fight," she recalls, referencing the climate of fear and violence that dominated the village at the time. People were being targeted and shot, she says. "Some even still have bullets lodged in their bodies."

In 2003, the self-recognition process of three Munduruku villages inside the Tapajós National Forest was already underway. This was roughly three hours by motorboat from Alter do Chão. These riverside communities had risen up against the narrative of whitening in hopes of reaffirming their identity and their right to stand up for what was theirs. As the Indigenous people of the Lower Tapajós River Basin often say, it was like an awakening from a deep sleep.

This movement spread throughout the region, influencing the Borari in Alter do Chão. A new age of communal organization had been born: meetings, trips to Brasília, and FUNAI conferences. "So we decided to create a council. But to us, as women, it didn't feel right to be led by men. We had a different way of thinking. And as you know, when a group isn't comfortable with the leadership it's got, for whatever reason, they'll create a new one: ours is a council of women only, and that council now represents the 180 families from Alter do Chão," Neca reflects.

What she's referring to is the Sapú Borari Women's Center. *Sapú*, as she explains, means "root." Neca portrays her mother as both festive and a fighter: terms that go hand-in-hand in the Indigenous Amazon region. Rituals are part of the intense life of these people, and the struggle to keep them from vanishing is a struggle for their own, unique way of life. Thus, as one of those responsible for the cultural part of the council, Dona Lusia occupied a position of importance when it came to communal ceremonies, cooking, rituals, craftwork, and storytelling.

Reclaiming Sairé, the village's traditional festival, also wouldn't have happened without Dona Lusia's efforts. "Sairé," says Neca, "was the god the Borari worshipped. But that part was banned by the priests in 1943." Dona Lusia had experienced the festivals of Sairé herself before they were banned by the Church.

"It wasn't until 1960 that people started getting together and holding the Sairé ceremony again. It was more about dances and rituals than prayer. There were maybe twenty people," Neca recalls. Dona Lusia was one of the "*comandos*" (as her daughter puts it) in charge of recovering the festival. "Our Indigenous rituals, our Amazonian *carimbó* dance. All the dances that we have here. She was all for prayer, but she was mostly concerned with the question of dancing. She always supported that part of it. She danced. And she enjoyed it."

Neca confirms that conversations with Dona Lusia were always filled with stories of the ancient times. And the one she most enjoyed telling was that of the Lago Verde do Muiraquitã, the community's lake. Dona Lusia made a point of visiting it shortly before she died, as if to bid it farewell. Today, the area is subject to aggressive real estate speculation.

It was on the banks of this lake in 2019, inside the Environmental Protection Area, that an intense fire destroyed an area equivalent to 1,647 soccer fields. Later that year, the Pará Civil Police accused members of the Alter do Chão volunteer brigade of being responsible, but in early 2020, state prosecutors dismissed the case, citing flaws in the investigation.

I'll end this obituary with the myth of the Lago Verde (the "Green Lake"), as told by Dona Lusia, through Neca Borari, to us. She talks about violence and disappearance, but also about the abiding belief in the moon and in the transfiguration of beings.

The lake is green because it has a history. Many years ago, when our ancestors lived here, a young Indian woman went missing from the village. And they went looking, they went on a search. The Borari people of Alter do Chão have the moon as their intermediary with Tupã, the creator.

Until today, in this age of real estate speculation, this invasion of other people, we would not have counted nine months to give birth, we would have counted nine moons. If you need to cut some straw to thatch the roof of your house, you can't do it under the moonlight. We only plant when the moon is strong. The fish are stronger under a full moon.

The people got together, all of the Borari people, to ask the moon to show them where the Indian girl was. And during the ritual, the moon answered them, saying yes, she would show them, she would give the girl back. So they went to the lake.

That afternoon, a great storm began to build. And they saw a tree rise up from the middle of the lake bearing colorful fruits that shone like lights. The tree moved, floating, along the river. After making a loop, it returned to the spot where it had begun. So the people went to see what was to be found.

Those bright fruits had been transformed. They had become green frogs, which together formed a large carpet stretching across the lake. Thus the name Lago Verde dos Muiraquitãs. The Indian girl's name was Naiá, and the tree was named Zineira, the tree of frogs.

In the Midst of a Pandemic, Belo Monte Is Suffocating the Xingu

In early 2020, when the new coronavirus arrived in Brazil, no one could have imagined that the Amazon would be the worst affected region. Covid-19 was supposed to follow the pattern of what unfolded in Europe earlier that year and to be concentrated in the major metropolitan areas in the southeast of the country. After all, that was the trend: In Europe it was the major cities, among them Paris, London, Madrid, and Brussels, that were worst affected by the pandemic.

Why should it be any different in Brazil? But soon enough the truth became clear. Cut to late September, when President Jair Bolsonaro gave a speech in the context of a historic increase in the number and extent of wildfires in the Amazon; he blamed these fires to the Indigenous and mestizo populations.

So detached from reality, this speech sparked indignation and rebellion among Indigenous peoples and environmentalists alike.

I had been covering the pandemic in Brazil for a few months when Bolsonaro gave this speech. I was particularly focused on the impact of the pandemic on Indigenous people and other traditional populations in the Amazon region, and on how it was not merely ignored but actively worsened by the president himself.

In late September, I was working as a scriptwriter for a podcast entitled *Scorched Earth: Stories of the Pandemic in the Amazon*. I and the production team decided to open the first episode with a discussion of Bolsonaro's speech. You could even say that the podcast was born of this tension between

Indigenous people and other traditional populations struggling to survive in the Amazon, on the one hand, and on the other the neglect and scorn of the federal government and other agents of the destruction.

One important question accompanied the podcasts. After five specific cases this boiled down to trying to understand what special features of the Amazon region that had allowed the new coronavirus to spread so easily and in such a deadly form, in 2020.

The fires, land grabbing, mining, and the expansion of soybean fields into the rainforest were all decisive factors in the Amazon's higher fatality rate from Covid-19 compared with other parts of the country. For Covid-19's impact on humans is like a magnifying glass; it accentuates preexisting inequalities. The devastation accumulates.

The data is changing at a dizzying rate. Still, though, there are several indications that the coronavirus is hitting the Amazon harder than other parts of the country.

One of the methodologies used to gauge the impact of an epidemic or a pandemic is excess mortality. This is when the death rate in a given place is higher than expected over a period of time compared to the historical average. According to data collected by Brazil's National Council of Health Secretaries for September 2020, the death rate in the state of Amazonas was 74 percent higher than expected. In São Paulo, the state most affected in terms of sheer numbers, the excess mortality was 15 percent.

Among the Indigenous peoples, the situation is even direr. During a report I worked on for the Thomson Reuters Foundation in mid-August 2020, I came across some surprising information: among Indigenous people in the Amazon the mortality rate from Covid-19 was over three times higher than that for the general population.

Historically there seems to be a pattern underlying the relationship between the Brazilian government and the Indigenous people. Diseases come and go, but cures don't. With Covid-19 the situation is even bleaker, because there is no cure. Many parts of the Amazon lack the sorts of hospital equipment necessary for proper treatment. The government rarely takes action, and, when it does, the results can be disastrous, with health workers themselves bringing the virus to Indigenous villages that had been trying to isolate themselves: a case we described in one of the podcast episodes.

This is why Indigenous organizations, *quilombolas*, and social movements representing the Afro-Brazilian population have come out to denounce this ongoing genocide—which seems, as I write these lines in April 2021, tragically far from over.

During one of the podcasts, I attempted to better understand how another, yet more marginalized Amazonian population is dealing with the Covid-19 pandemic: traditional riverside populations, for which we have even less data than we do for Indigenous people. For this reason, I decided to focus on those who were directly affected by the construction of the Belo Monte dam.

The Hydroelectric Dam

Belo Monte is the largest hydroelectric dam under construction in the world. And when it's ready, it will be the fourth largest in terms of power-generating capacity. Just behind Itaipu and China's Three Gorges and Xiluodu

dams. Everything here impresses with its greatness . . .
With a work of this huge extent, it's not the physical size
that most impresses and delights me. It's the size of the
benefits that it will bring to people's lives.

—DILMA ROUSSEFF, former president of Brazil,
during her reelection campaign, August 22, 2014.

Belo Monte is a hydroelectric dam built deep in the heart of the
Amazon rainforest. To be precise, it lies on the Xingu River, in
the state of Pará. It's a mega-structure that has spanned governments both left- and right-wing, democratic and authoritarian.

The dam's history is a long one. In the early 1970s, in the
midst of Brazil's so-called Years of Lead—its most troubled
period under military dictatorship—President Médici's government created the National Integration Plan for colonizing the Amazon, expanding the country's economic borders,
and—as the name states— bringing the country together.

The prevailing idea within the junta was that the Amazon
represented too much land for so few people. It went by another
name among the military leaders, one which aptly explains their
view of the region: "green desert," a term both synthetic and
aggressive, ignoring all the myriad forms of life that exist there.

Under the motto of "integrate, don't abdicate," the
construction of a" Brasil Grande" depended on a series
of developmental projects. Large highways, such as the
Transamazônica, the Perimetral Norte, and the Cuiabá-
Santarém carved up the Amazon region. It was all designed
to favor agricultural expansion, to attract workers from
other parts of the country, and to transform the rainforest
into plantations. Hydroelectric plants were a key part of
this major public works package, essential to generate the

energy that would be required for the country's so-called "economic miracle."

In 1975, Eletronorte, the dominant power generation company in northern Brazil, conducted the first studies on the Belo Monte project's feasibility. At the time, the facility was known as Kararaô, a name derived from the language of the Indigenous Kayapó people who still inhabit the Xingu River region. The project was the target of protests by both Indigenous peoples and environmental activists in the late 1980s. By 1989, when the redemocratization of Brazil was well underway, and in the wake of the most recently enacted Brazilian Constitution, the project was left in limbo.

Construction of the hydroelectric dam was only resumed in the 2000s. This triggered much controversy, with the country then under the administration of Luiz Inácio Lula da Silva (known popularly as "Lula"), leader of the Workers' Party and a fierce critic of the military dictatorship. Dilma Rousseff, then Lula's minister of mines and energy, was one of the principal champions of the plant. On May 5, 2016, having herself just been reelected to a second term as president, Rousseff—who had been persecuted and tortured by the Brazilian military dictatorship—inaugurated the commercial activities of the Belo Monte Dam.

Three and a half years later, in November 2019, the Belo Monte hydroelectric dam was opened again, to work at full capacity, by President Jair Bolsonaro.

In other words, whether you look at it from the left or the right of the political spectrum, the Belo Monte hydroelectric dam has always been used as a platform. In fact, much of Brazil's recent history could be told with Belo Monte as a focal point. But here I want to call attention to the people who live in this region, to understand how the construction of this dam has affected their lives, costing them their jobs, and forcing them to leave their homes.

Today, six years later, these people are now grappling with a lethal and highly transmissible virus while at the same time searching for ways to reshape their lives. One of them is Dona Lia.

Dona Lia

Lia Oliveira Lima Araújo does a little bit of everything. She works as a confectioner, as a farmer, and as a seller of goods such as semiplated jewelry, clothes, perfume, and various other things of that nature. It was in the construction of Altamira, a city on the banks of the Xingu River, that Dona Lia worked for decades as a brickmaker. She had churned out handmade bricks on the banks of a stream which was then flooded by the artificial lake created in 2015.

Altamira is the largest municipality in Brazil. It encompasses an area larger than Portugal or Switzerland. Both its forested region and its urban areas were badly affected by the construction of Belo Monte. Norte Energia, the company responsible for the dam's construction and operation, created an artificial lake to accumulate the water necessary to turn the hydroelectric plant's turbines, thereby flooding 478 square kilometers. This may not seem like much for a municipality the size of Portugal, but for the population living there, the transformation was devastating.

Among the flooded areas were the so-called baixões, or lowlands: neighborhoods of housing on stilts, riddled with streams and close to the Xingu River, including the riverside community where Dona Lia used to work. "It was a hard job, done out in the open," she reflects. "A craft that required a lot of effort, and which had a long history in our region. We used to say that, up until 2014, 60 percent of all construction in Altamira was done with handmade bricks from the brickyard."

While she doesn't glamorize this work, which was indeed demanding, she acknowledges the profound transformation that the end of this traditional labor brought about. As Dona Lia says, it was "an activity from which we could earn a living for our families," and also, "Despite being seasonal work, it could be passed down from parents to their children. In other words, they used to work part of the year, earning enough in the summer to live on during the winter. And that's what a job does, right? It meets your financial needs." Sometimes Dona Lia refers to the brickmakers in the third person, as if she weren't speaking about her own life.

She also says that she expected Norte Energia would help the brickmakers to find other brickyards where they could continue to work and not lose their income. But the reality that began to take shape in 2012 was quite different. The proposal to find the brickmakers alternative worksites has gone nowhere.

Many believed that the compensation money offered by Norte Energia would be enough for them to reorganize their lives. Dona Lia didn't agree. "A survey was taken of everyone who depended on this line of work. It included over three hundred people. And at the end of the day, not everyone was compensated. I wasn't really in favor of compensation, though, because I knew they wouldn't value our rights fairly enough to guarantee us a good amount of time to live with some dignity," she reflects. Without a job, the hard times were not far off. As Dona Lia says, "I felt so bad when I heard them complain about the situation they were in. I know it was a calamity."

For those who live in a city, in an urban center, it's difficult to grasp the import of Dona Lia's account. One must put in some imagination and effort in order to understand the impact of Belo Monte on the brickmakers' lives. These are craftsmen and women, people who had their workplaces—the places where they found the raw material for their bricks—flooded by the hydroelectric plant. The construction work to which they had dedicated their lives, the knowledge shared among the families, the source of their income and their very lifestyle as brickmakers: all of this had simply ceased to exist. Overnight, a new form of construction had arrived and taken over. And it is in the midst of this new turnaround, without adequate support from either the company responsible for the Belo Monte operational consortium or the government, that these people are now facing the Covid-19 pandemic.

After so many years without support, and with her source of income destroyed by the dam, the emergency aid that Bolsonaro's administration made available in mid-2020 is clearly vitally important to Dona Lia. This assistance also brought a surge in the Brazilian president's popularity, despite his catastrophic overall management of the pandemic. "All that's left to say is that there are many people thanking God today, right now, for the help they're receiving from the federal government, because Norte Energia didn't provide them with anything else," she says.

Invisible Communities

Carlos Gimenes is an anthropologist who was working on his master's degree while accompanying riverside populations in their daily lives around the time when Belo Monte was being built. Between late 2010 and mid-2015, he conducted over 150 interviews with people who were about to abandon major aspects of their lives in order to make room for the lake required by the hydroelectric dam. In the context of the dam's environmental licensing, Gimenes's role as an anthropologist overlapped with that of a researcher in the field of cultural heritage.

For Gimenes, the moment of the dam's construction can be described as "a moment of crisis, a moment of radical change from the previous way of life, when people's lives suddenly became very different and uncertain."

Years after the construction of Belo Monte, Gimenes returned to Altamira and, although he did not meet again with Dona Lia, one of his 150 original interviewees, he did encounter others with whom he had previously talked. They showed him a city trying to reinvent itself. Gimenes worked closely with these riverside residents who—along with Indigenous and *quilombola* communities—are among those worst affected by Belo Monte, and together form the multicultural territory that is the Amazon.

These are people who don't necessarily see themselves as Indigenous or *quilombola*, but who have traditional ways of life often organized around hunting, fishing, subsistence farming, or the local, small-scale selling of goods and crafts. Maintaining contact with nature is crucial for life along the riverbanks. In many cases, these people share cultural elements and beliefs with Indigenous and *quilombola* people. There is a constant flow of influences among these populations, including via songs, legends, and particular poetic forms.

Yet because these people aren't formally recognized as ethnic minorities, they aren't accorded the same rights. "The state of Brazil has no interest in and no structure for dealing with riverside communities," Carlos Gimenes explains. "In my view, the government should have treated these people the same, and offered them the same rights as other traditional people, for that's what they are."

Gimenes develops the comparison: "If we consider the Indigenous people who are legally recognized as traditional populations by the government to have been steamrolled by the Belo Monte, as they have been by so many other ventures, just imagine what happened to the riverside communities that don't share that distinction."

In the Amazon, the line separating those who are Indigenous from those who aren't always seems more fluid and more complicated than the government can handle. Constrained by tough and tightly worded legislation, its capacity to deal with the particular demands of riverside communities is acutely compromised. This is why I get the distinct impression that, throughout the Amazon region, when it comes to such conflicts, these people are left in the most precarious situation of all.

I have obtained excerpts from the July 2016 Civil Inquiry, signed by federal prosecutor Thais Santi Cardoso da Silva, one of the most active voices to challenge the procedures adopted during the construction of Belo Monte. The inquiry concerns a three-day visit, made in June 2015 by groups dedicated to defending human rights and by members of the academic community, to inspect riverine areas affected by the Belo Monte hydroelectric plant.

At that point, forced relocation was already underway. In other words, existing legislation regarding projects to be carried out on land occupied by traditional populations had not been respected. Thais Santi's inquiry observed:

> Since being removed from their traditional territories, riverside people find themselves in a state of "suspended

animation." Lacking any access to means of subsistence, they put up with suffering and exclusion, in a process that has changed so as not to change, and which provides daily evidence of the unsustainability of their lives. There's every indication that these groups will be forcibly moved yet again, using the wide range of violent tactics for which the Altamira region is well known.

Nonexistent in the eyes of the government, these populations were forced to move to the so-called RUCs, or "Collective Urban Resettlements"—neighborhoods created by Norte Energia on the outskirts of Altamira.

Collective Urban Resettlements

Igor Meireles is twenty-four years old, a student, and an activist with MAB, the "movement of people affected by dams," who grew up during this time of forced displacement and was himself directly affected by the Belo Monte. At the time of the removals, he was only fourteen, and living—like so many other riverside residents—in the *baixões*. "One of the groups who suffered the most from this transformation, this issue of relocation, was the fishermen," he says.

Igor goes on to explain how the involuntary relocation of riverside communities has uprooted their traditional way of life, not only in terms of the residents' proximity to one another and to Altamira's city center, but also by putting an end to their primary source of income and food: fishing. "This has become a matter of income exclusion as well as exclusion from daily sustenance in a community that routinely used to eat fish. We used to go down to the river and two hours later we'd come back with enough fish for a week, you know?" Igor explains.

For him, "These were real people who lived well, who knew a lot, and who really didn't have any problems bringing home food and generating income from fishing." Now, though, not only have the fishermen been sent to the outskirts of Altamira and so been forced to abandon the river, but, with the construction of Belo Monte, the hydrological flow of the Xingu has changed so drastically that, Igor says, "many species of fish have died out."

In the midst of the Covid-19 pandemic—a disease for which there are currently no effective treatments beside a vaccine, the distribution of which is still in its infancy in Brazil—these populations have faced the crisis far from the rivers and from their primary source of food.

How Belo Monte Is Suffocating the Xingu River

Fishermen from the Belo Monte do Pontal community, in the municipality of Anapu, which was also affected by the dam, saw their last "good catch" back in mid-August 2020. They spent seven days out fishing. They went upriver in canoes, as they traditionally do, up to the Volta Grande, a fluvial landscape stretching one hundred kilometers along a section of the Xingu River and situated just below the dam, which was off-limits to them so that it could power the turbines.

During that first trip after the months known as the "closed season"—when fishing is prohibited to allow the myriad species time to reproduce—they returned home with around two hundred kilograms of fish, enough to supply the community's needs and to generate some income for the fishermen.

In September 2020, with the Xingu running much drier, the same efforts yielded barely half as much. For subsequent trips, community members had to drive many miles in search of other fishing locations, for canoe access to their usual locations had been cut off by the drought. The water level was so low, in fact, that fishing had to be abandoned altogether.

"After August, everything was a loss," says Ana Laíde. She was born in a traditional fishing community herself, and works for the "Xingu Vivo" movement as a community organizer and on training for social education. The task to which she feels called is a challenging one: she works to strengthen the ties between riverside communities and Indigenous people affected by the Belo Monte hydroelectric dam.

In the pandemic one of Ana Laíde's main concerns is precisely the lack of food for populations dependent on fishing. "They're offering people bologna, and they're supposed to feed themselves with that. Malnutrition is built into the system," she says.

During the second half of 2020, the *piracema*, or spawning time, when the fish generally reproduce, never occurred at the Xingu's Volta Grande area, which is home to three Indigenous groups and twenty-five riverside communities. According to residents, this was because Belo Monte diverts too much water to the plant's reservoir.

Cleyson Juruna is a member of the Indigenous Juruna people, who identify themselves by the name of Yudjá. Two foods alternate as his principal dish: *pacu*, a fish, and *tracajá*, a species of turtle common in the Amazon region. But since 2015, Cleyson and others residing on the Paquiçamba Indigenous lands are no longer able to maintain this diet.

"The top part of the hydroelectric dam was full. But not here. All dried up! It was like summer all year long. The *curimatã* fish died with eggs in their bellies. There was just no place to spawn," Cleyson explains. In various parts of the Amazon, summer is a dry season with little rain and higher temperatures. At the Xingu's Volta Grande, fruits such as *sarão* (also known as *camu-camu*) and *caferana*, along with the fruit of the *arapari* tree, are fed upon by fish such as the *pacu*, *matrinxã*, and *surubim*. But during droughts, the fruits don't fall into the water but onto dry land, where they are of no use to the fish, he explains.

Moreover, with the decrease in water levels across the region, the fish are unable to spawn. Many are caught still holding roe that is almost decomposing and in the process of being reabsorbed into the fishes' bodies.

As a result, both income and food security are in a critical situation. "Our income, and the food we survived on, was the fish that came from that river. Our income fell 70 percent after the Xingu River was dammed," reflects Cleyson, who has been facing the Covid-19 pandemic with limited access to his primary source of food.

An Ecosystem Destroyed

The energy produced by the Belo Monte hydroelectric dam depends on diverting part of the Xingu River into "an artificial system, with the water being returned downstream, after the original course of the river takes a massive bend," explains Juarez Pezzuti, biologist and professor at the Center for High Amazonian Studies at the Federal University of Pará. "The greater the volume of water diverted, the greater the energy generated."

The problem, which is common among Amazonian rivers, is that the Xingu experiences "pulses of periodic inundations throughout its seasons of rising and high water." The life of the entire ecosystem, with its massive aquatic biodiversity, has come to depend on "the annual flooding of the vast wetland environments of the Xingu."

During this high-water season, between December and May, is when the fluctuating spates occur. Aquatic animals take advantage of these periodic floods to feed, and many species of fish reproduce. "These pulses of flooding are fundamental for aquatic fauna," Pezzuti explains.

Jansen Zuanon, a researcher with the National Institute for Amazonian Research (the INPA), explains how the Belo Monte Dam affects the reproduction cycle of fish and other species, destroying a unique area of sociobiodiversity. His research is centered on Amazonian fish populations, and his doctorate was focused on the ecology of the Xingu River basin. Zuanon takes two variables into account: the regularity and the predictability of water flow. "Both are important," he explains. "It's about how much water passes through the region, and for how long."

These two factors directly affect spawning. When Belo Monte restricts the volume of water flowing through the river, the fish are either trapped in stagnant pools that eventually dry up, or—when they are actually able to spawn—smaller fry return to the course of the river too early and become easy prey to larger species of fish.

Under normal circumstances, during the *piracema*—which comes from the Tupi words *pirá*, meaning "fish," and *sema*, meaning "exit"—fish swim upstream to their head-waters to spawn. But, as Zuanon explains, when the Xingu flowed naturally, "the fish were drawn downstream, towards the floodplains. That way the fry could return to the river only when they had grown big enough not to fit in the mouths of other fish."

This reproductive cycle has been significantly altered by Belo Monte. Zuanon describes how the hydroelectric plant adjusts the river's flow according to the demand for energy. In other words, "They are continually making adjustments. When less electricity is needed, they release a lot of water. Other times, they hold it back. So the river, which once followed a steady rhythm, is now completely unpredictable.

"They're operating a system that doesn't allow for these fluctuations to be perceived in good time, either by people or by aquatic organisms," he adds.

According to Zuanon, the models aiming to predict the effects of climate change on the Amazon show that the impact will vary depending on which part of the rainforest you're looking at: there will be more rain in the West, near the Andes, and greater dry periods in the East, right where the Xingu River basin is located. In the early 2000s, when the Belo Monte project resumed, based on this modeling as well as on historical data for flooding and droughts in the region, "it was already established that there wouldn't be enough water for Belo Monte to run throughout the year, especially during the summer months," he explains.

He points to the fact that the lowest high-water volume flow rate the Xingu experienced was 9,817 cubic meters per second back in April 1998. In other words, the smallest flood on record was higher than the best hydrograph ($8,000 \text{ m}^3/\text{s}$) proposed by Norte Energia. "And that sort of flow wouldn't even last a month," Zuanon says. "There would be no time for the ecological processes to take place."

Professor Juarez Pezzuti recalls that "in April, on the Xingu, the pulse reaches, on average, a peak of $20,000 \text{ m}^3/\text{s}$." For him, there's simply no way adequately to measure the adverse impact Belo Monte is having on the reproductive rates of animals such as fish and turtles.

Moreover, one look at the food security of Indigenous and riverside populations in the Xingu's Volta Grande suggests substantial losses. Pezzuti says that "fishermen are no longer able to catch the species traditionally important in their diet, forcing them to turn to others. They are consuming fewer and fewer fish, and this trend has been continuing since 2014."

Zuanon explains the difficulty of obtaining accurate measurement of species loss due to water being diverted into the hydroelectric turbines. Nobody knows precisely how large the areas no longer being flooded are, since much data is lacking from the models provided by Norte Energia. Zuanon calculates that 80 percent of all the local species of fish and plant life are at risk. In some specific locations, such as islands, the losses could reach 100 percent. "According to these hydrographs, the water will never get there. We did an on-the-spot check, which showed that 14,000 m³/s wasn't enough to flood some of the main islands where *piracema* should occur. The highest level predicted by the hydrograph is 11,000 m³/s. If that holds true, and the floodwaters never come, the loss will be 100 percent."

Zuanon warns that the situation created by Belo Monte "is pushing many species to the verge of extinction" and leaves them more vulnerable to other pressures, such as longer droughts, an increase in illegal gold mining in the Xingu basin, events outside the region, or even the construction of the Belo Sun mining project at Volta Grande.

And there are other concerns. "There could be a collapse in fishing," Zuanon says, "which would lead to serious food insecurity for the human populations that live there."

For Cleyson Juruna, the effects of the water's diversion in order to turn the Belo Monte turbines is felt at the dinner table. "Our main dish, which we used to eat every day, was the white *pacu*. But not anymore. Neither the quality nor the quantity is there anymore," he says.

Cleyson asserts that fish shortages are now recurring year after year. According to data from the national water agency, during the first three months of 2020, 66 percent of the water recommended for the Volta Grande was diverted to operate Belo Monte. This diversion was so great that the *piracema* never happened later that year, which is why Indigenous and riverside people protested against Norte Energia, the company responsible for Belo Monte, even managing to shut down the Transamazônica for five days in November 2020.

Igor Meireles, the young MAB activist who characterizes the times in which they're living as "a postconstruction hangover." But, considering what he sees going on everywhere he looks, he concludes: "Around here, things tend to get worse." Norte Energia did not answer the repeated questions I've sent them.

Epilogue: Writing Nearby

Much of what I have written in this book is about other people—people experiencing conflict and violence. Now, I'd like to offer a brief commentary on the personal anxieties that led me to embark on this journey. It's a way I can open up and explain the feelings that have motivated me in recent years: they are the genesis of everything you've just read.

Everything started quite simply. In mid-2016, all I wanted to do was travel around the Amazon and write. I wanted to try to understand what life means in this part of the planet, which is so much discussed and yet so poorly understood; to understand life and its powers of creation—powers that impressed me more with every conversation, every boat trip, every visit. But I also wanted to understand death and destruction.

At the time, having recently earned a master's degree in art history and anthropology, I was trying to consolidate a career along the lines of cultural centers and the visual arts. I made some great friends . . . the best friends I have to date. I learned a lot. But, somehow, I also felt discouraged—caught up in the somewhat self-absorbed game which characterized my experiences in this back-and-forth between academic life and cultural institutions. As thought-provoking as the issues were, I was missing something—something concrete.

I did my master's in Paris. I also worked as a bar guide there, carrying an almost-fluorescent orange umbrella around while shepherding British and American tourists through some truly awful bars around the Bastille district. I made just enough money to pay the bills and meet up with a few Latin American friends after work, which was usually around one in the morning. During the week I'd study, eat cheap and delicious food at Sri Lankan and Vietnamese restaurants (the smaller the establishment, the grimier the ambience, the more remote the location, and, of course, the spicier the food, the more affection we felt for the place), and work in the bars and restaurants, after which we would get together to drink and talk about literature, film, and our research.

Chepe, a Guatemalan friend, was studying the history of violence perpetrated by the dictatorship in his country and its consequences today. Andrés, one of the Colombians in our group, was investigating the impact of paramilitary activity in the Caribbean costal region. Inés, my best friend at the time, is Argentine, and was focusing on the literature and writing workshops she led for inmates serving time in Buenos Aires. For the Mexicans, the themes were violence, bodies, Indigenous revolts, and Zapatismo, among others. All of a sudden, I started to realize that my own research in art history, into conceptions of the future of modernity and the way time and politics were being articulated in works of contemporary art just . . . bored me.

I cultivated this sense of self-reflection for months, not out of envy, but as a question about the relevance of my research in a wider context. I am sure my discomfort was readily apparent to everyone. It was apparent to me, at least, which was enough to make me self-conscious about it. When I was defending my master's thesis, I clearly remember the vaguely tired gaze of one of the committee, Jacques Leenhardt, an art historian and Brazilianist. He began his questioning by complaining about three grammatical mistakes. "You can see this thesis wasn't written by a Frenchman," he said. "Well, of course it wasn't," I thought to myself. I was about to offer Monsieur Leenhardt a polite apology when, possibly realizing that I could offer little response to his initial comment, he amended it with another:

"Your text is fascinating, a bit rushed, perhaps, but nevertheless it's one of the best master's theses I've read. However, I get the impression that you're not really interested in art history per se, but more as an inquiry into *how to talk about politics*."

I don't know if that's exactly how he put it, but that's how it came across to me.

Board the boat. Tie up the hammock. Read. Chat with fellow travelers. Nap. Read. Nap. In storms, hold tight to one of the two masts that divide the deck. Descend the tight staircase belowdecks to eat. Go back to the hammock. Untie it. Arrive at the village. Tie the hammock up. Go out to fish. Go hunting. Conduct interviews. Get startled by a snake. A failed attempt at catching fish. A failed attempt to shoot a paca. Go back to the hammock. Wake up and listen to stories: of the ancients, of plants, of enchanted beings, of myths. A few days later, I board the boat again.

Sometimes I wonder how I came to this itinerant life, wandering through the Amazon, covering the conflicts in the areas I'm sent to by my editors in hopes I'll return safe and sound, with stories that are moderately well written, incisive, and which take into account the views of the people who live there. One of these editors, who to this day has trusted my work implicitly, and with whom I've collaborated many times, is Kátia Brasil. Our close-knit kinship is reflected in the number of texts reprinted here, and which were first published by the news agency *Amazônia Real*, which Kátia cofounded, along with Elaíze Farias.

Returning to these Amazonian wanderings is, as a photographer friend once put it, a bit like being a dog without an owner. I don't disagree. In fact, it's even possible to find a kind of pleasure in this life, even though the proliferating stories of conflict make it increasingly difficult to maintain a subjective stance.

I may have been overly influenced by books I read as a teenager. I've always been fond of displacement narratives, whether through time or space. But there were two writers in particular, both of whom born in the territory that is today the improbable nation of Belarus, who influenced me the most. Ryszard Kapuściński, who worked as a correspondent for the Polish Press Agency in the so-called Third World, and traveled to dozens of countries covering coups d'état, dictatorships, revolutions, wars, massacres, and the fall of rulers. As the narrator of so many crucial moments in the second half of the twentieth century, he developed his own methodology, projecting himself as an astute physiognomist of power and of the great political events as experienced "from the ground up": the way peasants and slum dwellers view revolutionary leaders, as opposed to the way industrialists and other figures of power see these processes. I devote more attention to this "geology of writing" in my book, *On the Escape Route*, so I won't dwell on it here.

The other key Belarusian influence in my life is Svetlana Alexievich, winner of the 2015 Nobel Prize for Literature. I remember reading somewhere that she had invented a new genre of fiction in which the novel was made up entirely of interviews and testimonies. That may be an exaggeration, but it does point to what I believe is the richest part of her work: diving deep into the lives of ordinary people in order to narrate major events in the history of the twentieth century, such as World War II, the collapse of Soviet socialism, and the Chernobyl nuclear disaster.

If I were to list all the works that I brought with me on these Amazonian wanderings, this book would not be ending anytime soon. There are Mexico's Cristina Rivera Garza and her experiments in search of writing that renders the pain of others; Tariq Ali's political engagement channeled via his passion for writing as denunciation; Susan Sontag's theoretical essays and intimate diaries; the lived sounds and sensations recreated by Natalia Ginzburg out of what has scarcely been seen, and which has almost no place; the nonfiction works of Antônio Callado and George Orwell (incidentally, to me, Orwell's greatest contributions to literature can be found here, not in his fiction); the rough, passionate world into which Anthony Bourdain invites us through his kitchens filled with workers who look more like pirates or war veterans than chefs or cooks; the attentive writing and ethical commitment of Eliane Brum; Elias Canetti, because you can always count on independent thought from this writer who truly understood the meaning of the word "essay"; the hours spent immersed in the magazine *Piauí*. And, finally, what for me is the best Brazilian essay ever written: *Tropical Truth*, by Caetano Veloso. This text is autobiographical, a memoir, critical, theoretical, emotional, humorous, and nonlinear—it is, in a word: elliptical.

To say that time passes differently in the Amazon would be an understatement. "You can catch a boat in Parauá on Monday," I'm told. I hop on a motorcycle and ride to Parauá through the rainforest only to find that the boat, in fact, only departs on

Wednesdays. "But don't worry," says Mercedes, an Indigenous health worker and spouse of *cacique* Braz, who is currently in the jungle. Unpredictability is the norm. A trip that should take six hours could easily last for ten.

Space and time move in mutual dependence. It's as if rivers, lakes, and forests can slow or even halt the passage of time as it's traditionally conceived: an arrow shot across a smooth surface. It's not like a car driving down the road. In the Amazon, time will take its time, at least as long as there are rivers and forests.

I savor these long hours on the boat. I'm not a fan of airplanes. I never have been, especially here in the Amazon, where flights are expensive and subject to turbulence stirred up by the massive cloud formations through which the tiny aircraft struggle to cleave. It's also on board the boats, during that extended travel time, where I learn the most about the different worlds that coexist in the rainforest.

It sometimes seems to me that people's lives in the Amazon take shape amid the friction between two worlds, between two ways of relating to the land. Or perhaps there's one way of life that connects with the land, and another that has pulled back from it, resulting in no connection at all. On the one side there are the connections of fishing, hunting, planting, and harvesting. An intimate experience of mutual education between the people and the land. On the other side are the impositions, formal and informal, of the market; a life defined by getting things "done." As such, it's not unlike the way the modern labor market is structured around the world . . . with one terrifying element in common: the iniquitous way in which enterprises big and small transform the people who live in these places into agents of the destruction of their own worlds.

The bond with the land has been severed, though this may not yet be permanent, given that it's not uncommon to hear about people who have left the big cities in the North and returned to their villages and communities of origin. To put it a better way, when this primary bond with the land is put on hold, those who once lived in the rainforest join a mass of people, both working and unemployed, who make up the bulk of the population in Amazonian cities. Crowds, as Elias Canetti said, tend to grow and become denser. This is their fundamental characteristic. The masses of Amazonian workers increase and become more compacted as the destruction of their territories goes on. It's no coincidence that one of the ways Canetti conceives of crowds is as a fire which spreads through everything, destroys everything, and reduces everything to ash. Thus Canetti offers even clearer analysis of what has happened, and continues to happen, across the globe: this is a machine that has long been working to remake Indigenous people into the urban poor.

In reports, columns, and even my own doctoral research in anthropology, there is one thing that has driven me more than any other during the past few years: the search for an appropriate way to relate the destruction of the Amazon rainforest, and the destruction of its myriad forms of life, from human to nonhuman and beyond human.

I have, then, developed a style afflicted with pain, of course, but one that also looks to reflect a certain exuberance, which may come as a surprise to some. It is my attempt to bring out not only a sense of the conflicts and fear, but also of the resistance exhibited by the Amazonian peoples' joyous fight for life, which is so often and so easily dismissed. An attempt to render the laughter and everyday humor with which they handle the most desperate situations; to render the richness of a world being destroyed and strategies for rebuilding it, like a guerrilla operating in silence: all but imperceptible, though not without strength and spirit.

Hence this search for a way to write with detail, with noise, in a said-but-almost-unsaid way. To not write about something. To not write with something. To hold my own world back even slightly. To try to articulate even a few of these other worlds. To find a style that creeps slowly, like a vine. To find, as the Vietnamese filmmaker and thinker Trinh T. Minh-ha puts it, a way of writing nearby.

Glossary

Açaí (*Euterpe oleracea*): A berry fruit that comes from a palm tree predominant in the Amazonian forest. Its name in Portuguese comes from the Tupi Indigenous languages. As fresh juice or "wine," as local Amazonians say, due to its fast fermentation process, it is mainly consumed in the Amazon region. But since the mid-1980s, açaí has started being used in other parts of Brazil as a frozen pulp and as an ingredient in different kinds of foods, cosmetics, and supplements. The fruit was promoted throughout the country as a superfood by the Gracie jiujitsu family. In the twenty-first century, açaí started conquering a broader international market as its nutritional characteristics as an antioxidant and source of vitamin E and iron, which significantly increased its value.

Amazônia Real: An independent, investigative, nonprofit journalism agency created in 2013 in Manaus in the state of Amazonas. The agency was founded and is directed by journalists Kátia Brasil and Elaíze Farias. The journalistic production is supported by a network of over thirty professionals, including reporters and photographers, who produce stories in Amazonas, Acre, Amapá, Maranhão, Mato Grosso, Rondônia, Roraima, Pará, Tocantins, Mato Grosso do Sul, São Paulo, and Rio de Janeiro. Most of the essays in this book were first published on the Amazônia Real website and edited by Kátia Brasil and Elaíze Farias.

Ariranha: A carnivorous mammal (*Pteronura brasiliensis*) of the mustelid family, it is found in the Amazon and central

Brazil and inhabits large rivers. It has a brown body, a flattened paddle-shaped tail, soft gray hair, and feeds on fish. Owing to its aggressiveness, it is also known as water-jaguar.

BAHSESE: A therapeutic technique developed hundreds and hundreds of years ago by Indigenous people from the Upper Rio Negro. According to João Paulo Lima Barreto, himself an Indigenous Tukano with a PhD in social anthropology, *bahsese* is "this model that is activated inside an element, it can either be water, tobacco, a cigarette, a nettle, in which the *kumu*, or the specialist, activates the healing principles contained in the vegetation. When he does this, he is not praying. He is evoking these principles to cure diseases. Therefore, he has to master the knowledge of plants and animals."

BAJARA: A simple kind of canoe used to transport fishermen and other people up and down the Brazilian Amazon and its tributaries.

CACIQUE, CACICA: An important Indigenous local leader. Its use comes from the word *kasik*, a term used by the Taino people from the Antilles, to designate a "chief." The Spanish first used the term *cacique* to designate the "Taino political system." This form of chiefdom isn't equivalent to state political forms of organization, as there is no administrative staff or permanent army. Despite the use of the term *cacique* by European colonizers throughout America, each Indigenous group from the many different regions of the continent had a name and conception for its leaders. Its use in the feminine (*cacica*) is a recent victory for Indigenous women's political articulations.

CARIMBÓ: A traditional dance from the Amazonian state of Pará, with Indigenous roots and influenced by Afro-Brazilian and Portuguese rhythms. It is both the name of the dance and the drums used to create the beat.

CARPI: A hallucinogenic made with liana bark, ground in a pestle, mixed with cold water, strained, and drunk by Indigenous people. It is known as a bitter, indigestible tea that enables communication with nonhuman beings and the receiving of knowledge. It was forbidden by Catholic missionaries in the region of the Upper Rio Negro and has only been reimplemented by Indigenous communities during the last few decades.

CAXIRI: Also known as cauim, it is an alcoholic beverage made from fermented manioc. It is a central element in Indigenous festivals, rituals, and political moments.

COMUNIDADE: A community, in the Amazonian context, usually refers to a group of people that live together and share some cultural and familial relations. Just as a territory occupied by a specific Indigenous people may consist of different communities or villages, a protected area may be formed by several communities. The same is true with a *quilombo*.

CRIOLLO: A term used in Hispanic colonies throughout the Americas since the beginnings of the colonization to refer to those born in the New World but with European ancestry.

In modern times, it has also been used in some Spanish-speaking countries throughout Latin America to refer to the general population, which originated throughout the historical miscegenation of European, Indigenous, and Afro-American peoples. In this sense, it can be used as a way to refer to the general population, as opposed to the Indigenous minorities, as is the case in the story "An Afternoon with Venezuelans at the Manaus Bus Terminal Overpass."

In Brazil, however, the use of the word *crioulo* has a different meaning. When used by a white person to refer to a Black person, it usually confers a racist intent. Nevertheless, there is also an anti-racist revindication and ownership of the term by Afro-Brazilians.

CUPUAÇU: An elegant tree (*Theobroma grandiflorum*) native to the Amazon, with long branches, tapering to a point, with rusty leaves on the bottom, red flowers, and large capsular fruits that are smooth, egg-shaped, and edible. The pulped fruit of these trees is used in juices, jams, sweets, and ice creams, and the seeds, similar to those of cocoa, are used to create a kind of chocolate known as *cupulate*.

DROGAS DO SERTÃO: The *sertão* drugs bring together the different types of spices (plants, roots, seeds, fruits, medicinal herbs, etc.) that were marketed by colonial Brazil in the sixteenth and seventeenth centuries. Some scholars refer to this moment of Brazilian history as the "Cycle of Drogas do Sertão."

Sertão here predominantly means "forests." Europeans considered products such as cacao, Brazil nuts, guaraná, pau-clove, and urucú as "new spices."

With the presence of other Europeans such as the French, English, Dutch, and Spanish engaged in smuggling at the mouth of the Amazon River, the Portuguese began exploratory ventures into the jungle to expand their trade dominance. In this context, pioneers known as *Bandeirantes* entered the forest to explore the land, apprehend fugitive slaves, and capture Indigenous people.

With the beginning of the cultivation of sugar cane during the seventeenth century, which quickly became Brazil's primary export, the exploitation of "Drogas do Sertão" fell into decline.

EXTRACTIVE RESERVE: Extractive reserves are areas used by traditional populations whose survival is based on extractivism, subsistence farming, and small-scale raising of domestic animals. In Brazil, an extractive reserve is managed by a deliberative council, chaired by the body responsible for its administration, and made up of representatives of public bodies, civil society organizations, and traditional populations residing in the area.

Federal extractive reserves are managed by the Chico Mendes Institute for Biodiversity Conservation (ICMBio).

ENCANTADO: Among Indigenous peoples and rural populations influenced by their knowledge and cultural background, the "enchanted" are nonhuman beings, endowed with powers and knowledge unknown to humans. They can inhabit the sky, the jungles, the waters, the bottom of the rivers, certain rock formations, or sacred places. The term can also be used as a verb (*se-encantou*—someone "was enchanted") to refer to a way of disappearing from this plane of existence in a way quite different from death. For example, important shamans do not die but rather "are enchanted." In this same sense, within the context of Indigenous people's struggle for their self-determination, it is also possible to hear Indigenous people saying, among themselves, that when an important Indigenous leader dies the leader 'is enchanted.'

FAZENDA: A rural property intended for the practice of agriculture and/or livestock. In Brazil, farms have historically been places where the monoculture plantation system was developed using enslaved labor. For centuries fazendas were the center of political power, as if each great farmer was himself a small feudal lord.

Although this structure has been broken during the country's process of modernization, there are some elements that still remain to this day: it is common to read investigative reports about farms involved in cases of violence against neighboring populations or forcing people to work in conditions analogous to slavery. In addition, large farmers are still important political forces in their regions with family members serving as politicians and judges. And beyond that, fazendeiros have enormous relevance in national politics, with broad representation both in the Chamber of Deputies and in the Senate.

FUNAI: Brazil's National Indian Foundation is linked to the Ministry of Justice. FUNAI is responsible for promoting studies of identification and delimitation, demarcation, land tenure regularization, and registration of lands traditionally occupied by Indigenous peoples. It is also in charge of monitoring and inspecting Indigenous lands. In recent years, the foundation has faced pressure from military, evangelist, and rural groups interested in exploring Indigenous territories.

GAÚCHO: A person born in the state of Rio Grande do Sul. They are used in parts of the Amazon to refer to soy farmers, as many of the first soy farmers came from the Rio Grande do Sul.

INCRA: The National Institute for Colonization and Agrarian Reform is a federal autocracy whose priority mission is to implement agrarian reform and carry out the national land order. As the institute oversees huge amounts of land in every corner of Brazil, it is often pressured by influential local farmers. From time to time, cases of corruption scandals and land grabbing occur that involve the institute's functionaries.

JARARACA: A name common to several venomous snakes of the *Bothrops* genus, of the viperid family, found in South America, and known for their triangular heads and tapered, rattleless tails.

KUMU, KUMUÃ (SING, PL): This is the way a Tukano refers to a shaman. A *kumu* is a specialist, an important connoisseur of the mythologies and ritual practices acquired through years of training.

One of the main roles of the *kumu* lies in preventing disease and misfortune. He is an expert in the art of "blowing" and has the power to convert usually dangerous foods like fish and game meat into regular food. He has a prominent role in rites of passage and performs the main ceremonies at birth, initiation, and death. It is the *kumu* that names newborn babies, and it is he who conducts rites of passage. Such transitions involve a necessary and potentially beneficial contact between the living, the spirits, and the dead. This contact can be dangerous, and it is the *kumu* who takes responsibility for protecting people. Another important role of the *kumu* is to preside over dance parties, *caxiri* parties, and ceremonial gatherings where they conduct and supervise rituals in which instruments are played: rituals that involve direct contact with dead ancestors.

The *kumu* were considered by Catholic missionaries to be sorcerers and were therefore persecuted.

MANIOC: A species of tuberous plant in the Euphorbiaceae family. The name given to the stem of the manioc tree is *maniva*, which, cut into pieces, is used in planting. It is a shrub that originated in remote southwestern Amazonia and that, long before the arrival of Europeans in America, had already spread, as a food crop, to Mesoamerica, in what is now Guatemala and Mexico.

After being treated at high temperatures, which makes them lose their toxicity, the roots are used to produce flour, tapioca, starch, *beijus*, and other foodstuff. Together with fishes and game meat, it is the primary ingredient in Indigenous cuisine.

Muiraquitãs: A word from the Tupi linguistic tree that designates an artifact usually carved in stone, which can function as an amulet and symbol of power, mostly in the shape of a frog, but also of a turtle or snake. Its use is found in different parts of the Amazon, but it is particularly common in the Tapajós River region, and the Upper Rio Negro.

There are several myths related to the *muiraquitãs*, such as that of the warrior women who had no husbands, the *icamiabas* (origin of the myth of the Amazonas women), who produced the *muiraquitãs* as part of their rituals.

In a major work of Brazilian literature, *Macunaíma* (1928) by Mário de Andrade, the narrative plot revolves around the attempt to recover a *muiraquitã*.

Pajé: A generic word in Portuguese to refer to an Indigenous shaman. Each Indigenous language may have its own manner of referring to its shaman, but may use the term *pajé* when talking to non-Indigenous people. At the same time, some Brazilian Indigenous groups call their shamans *pajés* within their own communities, especially among Tupi-speaking peoples.

Quilombo, quilombola: A *quilombo* is the term traditionally describing a group of enslaved people who escaped and formed a community, as well as their descendants. A more contemporary interpretation would define *quilombolas* as self-defined ethnic/racial groups, with their own historical backgrounds and documented Black ancestry related to the historic fight against racism.

REAL, REAIS (SING, PL): The Brazilian currency adopted in 1994 after several monetary changes. The "Plano real," which established *real* as the Brazilian coin, is known for its success in controlling inflation. Despite the relative stability of the currency compared to previous variations, it has been devaluated significantly since the economic and political changes that began in 2015/2016.

TITLES DONA, SEU, AND SENHOR: Respectful ways of referring to someone older in much of Brazil. "Dona" (feminine noun) and "Senhor" (masculine noun, which is commonly used in its abbreviation form, "Seu").

WAI-MAHSÃ: According to João Paulo Barreto Tukano, "*Wai-Mahsã* is any human being who is not in contact with you. They're known to exist but otherwise have no connection with you. So, as a stranger, someone you don't know, he is called *Wai-mahsã*. Thus, in the time when we had no contact with non-Indigenous people, you were also called *Wai-Mahsã*." João Paulo also considers the *Wai-Mahsã* as invisible humans, "owners" of the environment, of places or animals: the water, the fish, the forest. He believes anthropologists have wrongly translated the term as "fish-person," which is nothing more than the literal translation.

About the Texts

"A Forest in Flames" was originally published by the magazine *Piseagrama* in March 2020. This text is part of the doctoral research in social anthropology being conducted by the author in the Lower Tapajós River Basin on the destruction of Indigenous territories and their forms of resistance. This research is supported by the São Paulo Research Foundation (FAPESP).

"Brazilians and Venezuelans: A Chronicle of Hatred and Compassion" was originally published in *Agência Pública* in September 2018 as "Brasileiros e venezuelanos: uma crônica de ódio e compaixão."

"The Life and Death of a Minke Whale in the Amazon" was originally published in *Amazônia Real* in December 2017 as "Vida e Morte de uma Baleia-Minke no Rio Tapajós."

"An Afternoon with Venezuelans at the Manaus Bus Terminal Overpass" was originally published in *Amazônia Real* in March 2019 as "Uma tarde junto aos venezuelanos no viaduto da rodoviária de Manaus."

"The Self-Demarcation of Tupinambá Indigenous Land in the Lower Tapajós River Basin" was originally published in *Nexo Jornal* in January 2017 under the title "A autodemarcação da Terra Indígena Tupinambá no Baixo Tapajós."

"Anamã: Six Months Underwater, Six Months on Dry Land" was originally published in *Amazônia Real* in May 2019 as "Anamã, cidade que vive o extremo da cheia e da seca."

"The Poison Fields" was originally published by *Le Monde Diplomatique Brasil* in February 2020. The article is accompanied by a video and photo essay created by Bruce Kelly, which can be viewed here: youtu.be/04Is5kjt8CQ. This material was produced thanks to the support of the Rainforest Journalism Fund in partnership with the Pulitzer Center.

"'Nature Herself Is Drying Up': A *Quilombo* on the Marajó Archipelago Feels the Impact of Rice Paddies amid Turbulent Times" was originally published by *Amazônia Real* in April 2020. The article is accompanied by a video and photo essay created by Cícero Pedrosa Neto, which can be viewed here: youtu.be/sNcYIviawXA. This material was produced with the support of Reporters Without Borders, the largest international organization dedicated to defending freedom of the press, understood as the fundamental human right to inform and to be informed.

"The *Kumuã* of the Upper Rio Negro and the Decolonization of Indigenous Bodies" was originally published in *Amazônia Real* in August 2019 in two parts, titled "Os kumuã do Alto Rio Negro: especialistas da cura indígena" and "A picada da jararaca e o desprezo ao conhecimento dos kumuã do Alto Rio Negro."

"Between the Festival and the Fight: The Life of the First Indigenous Person in Brazil to Die from COVID-19" was originally published by *Amazônia Real* in April 2020 as "Entre festa e luta, a vida da indígena Borari vítima da Covid-19."

"In the Midst of a Pandemic, Belo Monte is Suffocating the Xingu" is comprised of different materials. It is based on the fifth episode ("The Ones Hit by Belo Monte") of the podcast *Scorched Earth: Stories of the Pandemic in the Amazon*, conducted by Le Monde Diplomatique Brasil with support from the Rainforest Journalism Fund in partnership with the Pulitzer Center and produced by Trovão Mídia. To this I added excerpts from articles I wrote after the podcast, including "Deviating Water to Belo Monte Impacting Fish Breeding in the Xingu River" (published on January 21, 2021 by InfoAmazonia) and "Belo Monte Is Suffocating the Xingu River" (published on March 19, 2021, also by InfoAmazonia).

Acknowledgments

It is the people who, themselves, make up this book that I must thank first and foremost. The people who decided to open a part of their lives to us during times of political tension, forest devastation, and crimes against the environment. They were courageous enough to share delicate situations with a total stranger. They welcomed me into their homes, shared fish, flour, and fruit with me, believing that something good might actually come from the telling of these stories.

This book brings together reports, columns, and stories that couldn't have been written without the support of media outlets committed to a critical reflection on what is happening in the Amazon today. Kátia Brasil and Elaíze Farias, cofounders of the *Amazônia Real* news agency and experienced reporters themselves, are two people with whom I've learned the most about the Amazon. It's no coincidence that the majority of the texts reprinted here were first published on the *Amazônia Real* platform. Natalia Viana, Marina Amaral, and Thiago Domenici, of *Agência Pública*, had faith in the idea of an article about the border between Brazil and Venezuela. Marina Menezes, of *Nexo Jornal*, was responsible for publishing the essay-report I wrote about the Tupinambá efforts to self-demarcate their land, which was the first piece I wrote while in the Amazon. The Pulitzer Center, together with the Rainforest Journalism Fund, supported my investigation into the lives of traditional farmers surrounded by soy in the Lower Tapajós River. I must also thank Luís Brasilino and Bianca Pyl, at *Le Monde Diplomatique Brasil*, for his editorial oversight. And

Reporters Without Borders supported the investigation at the Marajó Archipelago. I also want to thank the editors of *Revista Piseagrama*, especially Felipe Carnevalli De Brot.

I am also grateful to the Pulitzer Center and the Rainforest Journalism Fund for the support for the podcast on the impact of the covid-19 pandemic in the Amazon, which I tried to convert into an essay here. I want to thank Verónica Goyzueta and Nora Moraga-Lewy (with Pulitzer Center), Ana Bonomi and José Orenstein (with Trovão Mídia) and Juliana Mori (with InfoAmazônia), and also the team of Le Monde Diplomatique Brazil I've just mentioned for this our long-lasting partnership.

Ismar Tirelli Neto read, commented, and reflected with me on various passages from this book, pointing out ways through and enhancing certain images (any errors or exaggerations are, of course, exclusively my own). The book's illustrations, drawn by the Indigenous artist Gustavo Caboco, deserve equal parts attention and affection. It was Laura Daviña, editor and designer at Publication Studio São Paulo, who thought of inviting Gustavo to participate.

This book's first publication of this due to Laura Daviña's vision, but also to the vision of another Laura—Laura Viana. The book is the result of our open dialogue about the texts coupled with a detailed eye for the possibilities of editing and design.

For the English edition, I would like to thank Daniel Slager for his editing and Ezra E. Fitz for his translation. Daniel took the brave decision to publish this material in English, for a wider public beyond Portuguese readers. This only became possible due to the precise and creative work of Ezra E. Fitz, who faced a particular challenge: translating into English specific Amazonian expressions, and plant and animal names—a whole world recreated in another language. Sophie Lewis did an extraordinary and thorough edit of the text. The whole team of Milkweed Editions, especially Lee Oglesby and Broc Rossell, dedicated a lot of energy to give life to this book in English. All of this only became possible after a suggestion by Mary Austin Speaker, who is also responsible for the beautiful cover of this book.

Fábio Zuker

Fábio Zuker has been a Pulitzer Center grantee three times, has written articles for *National Geographic Brasil*, *Revista Piauí*, *Le Monde Diplomatique Brasil*, *Agência Pública*, *InfoAmazonia*, and *Nexo Jornal*, among others, and is a frequent contributor to *Amazônia Real* and Thomson Reuters Foundation. He holds a master's degree from Paris's School for Advanced Studies in Social Sciences and is a PhD candidate in Social Anthropology at the University of São Paulo.

Natasha Parker

Ezra E. Fitz is the translator of *The Life and Death of a Minke Whale in the Amazon*. His translations of contemporary Latin American literature by Alberto Fuguet, Eloy Urroz, and others have been praised by the *New York Times*, *the Washington Post*, *the New Yorker*, and *The Believer*, among other publications. Fitz has worked with Grammy-winning musician Juanes, Emmy-winning journalist Jorge Ramos, and the king of soccer himself, Pelé. Awarded grants from the Mexican National Fund for Culture and Arts (FONCA), he was a 2010 Resident at the Banff International Literary Translation Centre, and a 2019 Peter Taylor Fellow with the Kenyon Review Literary Translation Workshop. He lives with his wife and children in Spring Hill, Tennessee.

milkweed
editions

Founded as a nonprofit organization in 1980, Milkweed
Editions is an independent publisher. Our mission is to
identify, nurture and publish transformative literature, and
build an engaged community around it.

Milkweed Editions is based in Bdé Óta Othúŋwe
(Minneapolis) within Mní Sota Makhóčhe, the traditional
homeland of the Dakhóta people. Residing here since time
immemorial, Dakhóta people still call Mní Sota Makhóčhe
home, with four federally recognized Dakhóta nations and
many more Dakhóta people residing in what is now the state
of Minnesota. Due to continued legacies of colonization,
genocide, and forced removal, generations of Dakhóta
people remain disenfranchised from their traditional
homeland. Presently, Mní Sota Makhóčhe has become a
refuge and home for many Indigenous nations and peoples,
including seven federally recognized Ojibwe nations. We
humbly encourage our readers to reflect upon the historical
legacies held in the lands they occupy.

milkweed.org

Milkweed Editions also gratefully acknowledges sustaining support from our Board of Directors; the Alan B. Slifka Foundation and its president, Riva Ariella Ritvo-Slifka; the Amazon Literary Partnership; the Ballard Spahr Foundation; *Copper Nickel*; the McKnight Foundation; the National Endowment for the Arts; the National Poetry Series; the Target Foundation; and other generous contributions from foundations, corporations, and individuals. Also, this activity is made possible by the voters of Minnesota through a Minnesota State Arts Board Operating Support grant, thanks to a legislative appropriation from the arts and cultural heritage fund. For a full listing of Milkweed Editions supporters, please visit milkweed.org.

Interior Design by Mary Austin Speaker and Tijqua Daiker

Typeset in Fournier

Fournier is a typeface created by the Monotype Corporation in 1924, based on types cut in the mid-eighteenth century by Pierre-Simon Fournier, a French typographer. The specific cuts used as a reference for Fournier are referred to as "St Augustin Ordinaire" in Fournier's influential *Manuel Typographique*, published in 1764 in Paris.